VA

ALSO BY GLENNON DOYLE

Carry On, Warrior

Love Warrior

untamed

untamed

glennon doyle

the dial press
new york

Copyright © 2020 by Glennon Doyle

All rights reserved.

Published in the United States by The Dial Press, an imprint of Random House, a division of Penguin Random House LLC, New York.

THE DIAL PRESS is a registered trademark and the colophon is a trademark of Penguin Random House LLC.

Acknowledgment is made to M. Peck Scott (*The Road Less Traveled*) and William James (*The Varieties of Religious Experience*) for their presentation of the "the unseen order of things."

In addition, acknowledgment and appreciation is expressed to Professor Randall Balmer, whose 2014 *Politico* article "The Real Origins of the Religious Right" informed and impacted the "Decals" chapter of this book.

Grateful acknowledgment is made to the following for permission to reprint previously published material:
Daniel Ladinsky: "Dropping Keys" adapted from the Hafiz poem by Daniel Ladinsky from *The Gift: Poems by Hafiz* by Daniel Ladinsky, copyright © 1999 by Daniel Ladinsky. Used with permission.
W. W. Norton & Company, Inc.: Five lines from "A Secret Life" from *Landscape at the End of the Century* by Stephen Dunn, copyright © 1991 by Stephen Dunn. Used with permission of W. W. Norton & Company, Inc.
Writers House LLC: Excerpt from "Letter from a Birmingham Jail" by Dr. Martin Luther King Jr., published in TheAtlantic.com. This article appears in the special MLK issue print edition with the headline "Letter From Birmingham Jail" and was published in the August 1963 edition of *The Atlantic* as "The Negro Is Your Brother," copyright © 1963 by Dr. Martin Luther King Jr. and copyright renewed 1991 by Coretta Scott King. Reprinted by arrangement with The Heirs to the Estate of Martin Luther King Jr., c/o Writers House as agents for the proprietor New York, NY.

Library of Congress Cataloging-in-Publication Data
Names: Doyle, Glennon, author.
Title: Untamed / Glennon Doyle.
Description: New York : The Dial Press, 2020.
Identifiers: LCCN 2019047945 (print) | LCCN 2019047946 (ebook) |
    ISBN 9781984801258 (hardcover) | ISBN 9781984801265 (ebook)
Subjects: LCSH: Doyle, Glennon, 1976– | Married women—United
    States—Biography. | Wambach, Abby, 1980– —Family. | Lesbians—United
    States—Biography. | Christian biography.
Classification: LCC CT275.M469125 A3 2020 (print) |
    LCC CT275.M469125 (ebook) | DDC 306.89/3—dc23
LC record available at https://lccn.loc.gov/2019047945
LC ebook record available at https://lccn.loc.gov/2019047946

PRINTED IN THE UNITED STATES OF AMERICA ON ACID-FREE PAPER

randomhousebooks.com

20 19 18 17 16 15 14 13 12

For every woman resurrecting herself.
For the girls who will never be buried.

Mostly, for Tish.

contents

cheetah

Two summers ago, my wife and I took our daughters to the zoo. As we walked the grounds, we saw a sign advertising the park's big event: the Cheetah Run. We headed toward the families scouting out their viewing spots and found an empty stretch along the route. Our youngest, Amma, hopped up on my wife's shoulders for a better view.

A peppy blond zookeeper in a khaki vest appeared. She held a megaphone and the leash of a yellow Labrador retriever. I was confused. I don't know much about animals, but if she tried to convince my kids that this dog was a cheetah, I was getting a Cheetah Run refund.

She began, "Welcome, everybody! You are about to meet our resident cheetah, Tabitha. Do you think this is Tabitha?"

"Nooooo!" the kids yelled.

"This sweet Labrador is Minnie, Tabitha's best friend. We introduced them when Tabitha was a baby cheetah, and we raised Minnie alongside Tabitha to help tame her. Whatever Minnie does, Tabitha wants to do."

The zookeeper motioned toward a parked jeep behind her. A pink stuffed bunny was tied to the tailgate with a fraying rope.

She asked, "Who has a Labrador at home?"

Little hands shot into the air.

"Whose Lab loves to play chase?"

"Mine!" the kids shouted.

"Well, Minnie loves to chase this bunny! So first, Minnie will do the Cheetah Run while Tabitha watches to remember how it's done. Then we'll count down, I'll open Tabitha's cage, and she'll take off. At the end of the route, just a hundred meters that way, there will be a delicious steak waiting for Tabitha."

The zookeeper uncovered Tabitha's cage and walked Minnie, eager and panting, to the starting line. She signaled to the jeep, and it took off. She released Minnie's leash, and we all watched a yellow Lab joyfully chase a dirty pink bunny. The kids applauded earnestly. The adults wiped sweat from their foreheads.

Finally it was time for Tabitha's big moment. We counted down in unison: "Five, four, three, two, one . . ." The zookeeper slid open the cage door, and the bunny took off once again. Tabitha bolted out, laser focused on the bunny, a spotted blur. She crossed the finish line within seconds. The zookeeper whistled and threw her a steak. Tabitha pinned it to the ground with her oven-mitt paws, hunkered down in the dirt, and chewed while the crowd clapped.

I didn't clap. I felt queasy. The taming of Tabitha felt . . . familiar.

I watched Tabitha gnawing that steak in the zoo dirt and thought: *Day after day this wild animal chases dirty pink bunnies down the well-worn, narrow path they cleared for her. Never looking left or right. Never catching that damn bunny, settling instead for a store-bought steak and the distracted approval of sweaty strangers. Obeying the zookeeper's every command, just like Minnie, the Lab she's been trained to believe she is. Unaware that if she remembered her wildness—just for a moment—she could tear those zookeepers to shreds.*

When Tabitha finished her steak, the zookeeper opened a gate that led to a small fenced field. Tabitha walked through and the gate closed behind her. The zookeeper picked up her megaphone again and asked for questions. A young girl, maybe nine years old, raised her hand and asked, "Isn't Tabitha sad? Doesn't she miss the wild?"

"I'm sorry, I can't hear you," the zookeeper said. "Can you ask that again?"

The child's mother said, louder, "She wants to know if Tabitha misses the wild."

The zookeeper smiled and said, "No. Tabitha was born here. She doesn't know any different. She's never even seen the wild. This is a good life for Tabitha. She's much safer here than she would be out in the wild."

While the zookeeper began sharing facts about cheetahs born into captivity, my older daughter, Tish, nudged me and pointed to Tabitha. There, in that field, away from Minnie and the zookeepers, Tabitha's posture had changed. Her head was high, and she was stalking the periphery, tracing the boundaries the fence created. Back and forth, back and forth, stopping only to stare somewhere beyond the fence. It was like she was remembering something. She looked regal. And a little scary.

Tish whispered to me, "Mommy. She turned wild again."

I nodded at Tish and kept my eyes on Tabitha as she stalked. I wished I could ask her, "What's happening inside you right now?"

I knew what she'd tell me. She'd say, "Something's *off* about my life. I feel restless and frustrated. I have this hunch that everything was supposed to be more beautiful than this. I imagine fenceless, wide-open savannas. I want to run and hunt and kill. I want to sleep under an ink-black, silent sky filled with stars. *It's all so real I can taste it.*"

Then she'd look back at the cage, the only home she's ever known. She'd look at the smiling zookeepers, the bored spectators, and her panting, bouncing, begging best friend, the Lab.

She'd sigh and say, "I should be grateful. I have a good enough life here. It's crazy to long for what doesn't even exist."

I'd say:

Tabitha. You are not crazy.

You are a goddamn cheetah.

part one
caged

sparks

Four years ago, married to the father of my three children, I fell in love with a woman.

Much later, I watched that woman drive away from my home to meet with my parents and share her plan to propose to me. She thought I didn't know what was happening that Sunday morning, but I knew.

When I heard her car return, I settled into the couch, opened a book, and tried to slow my pulse. She walked through the door and directly toward me, bent down, kissed my forehead. She pushed my hair aside and took a deep breath of my neck, like she always does. Then she stood up and disappeared into the bedroom. I walked to the kitchen to pour some coffee for her, and when I turned around, she was right there in front of me, down on one knee, holding a ring. Her eyes were certain and pleading, wide and laser focused, sky blue, bottomless.

"I couldn't wait," she said. "I just could not wait another minute."

Later, in bed, I laid my head on her chest while we talked about her morning. She'd told my parents, "I love your daughter and grandchildren like I've never loved before. I've spent my entire life searching and preparing myself for them. I promise you that I will love and protect them forever." My mother's lip quivered with fear and courage as she said, "Abby. I have not seen my daughter this alive since she was ten years old."

Much else was said that morning, but that first response from my mother jumped out at me like a sentence in a novel begging to be underlined:

I have not seen my daughter this alive since she was ten years old.

My mother watched the spark in my eyes fade during my tenth year on Earth. Now, thirty years later, she was witnessing the return of that spark. In the past few months, my entire posture had changed. I looked regal to her. And a little scary.

After that day, I began to ask myself: *Where did my spark go at ten? How had I lost myself?*

I've done my research and learned this: Ten is when we learn how to be good girls and real boys. Ten is when children begin to hide who they are in order to become what the world expects them to be. Right around ten is when we begin to internalize our formal taming.

Ten is when the world sat me down, told me to be quiet, and pointed toward my cages:

These are the feelings you are allowed to express.
This is how a woman should act.
This is the body you must strive for.
These are the things you will believe.
These are the people you can love.
Those are the people you should fear.
This is the kind of life you are supposed to want.

Make yourself fit. You'll be uncomfortable at first, but don't worry—eventually you'll forget you're caged. Soon this will just feel like: life.

I wanted to be a good girl, so I tried to control myself. I chose a personality, a body, a faith, and a sexuality so tiny I had to hold my breath to fit myself inside. Then I promptly became very sick.

When I became a good girl, I also became a bulimic. None of us can hold our breath all the time. Bulimia was where I exhaled. It was where I refused to comply, indulged my hunger, and expressed my fury. I became animalistic during my daily binges. Then I'd drape myself over the toilet and purge because a good girl must stay very small to fit inside her cages. She must leave no outward evidence of her hunger. Good girls aren't hungry, furious, or wild. All of the things that make a woman human are a good girl's dirty secret.

Back then, I suspected that my bulimia meant that I was crazy. In high school, I did a stint in a mental hospital and my suspicion was confirmed.

I understand myself differently now.

I was just a caged girl made for wide-open skies.

I wasn't crazy. I was a goddamn cheetah.

When I saw Abby, I remembered my wild. I wanted her, and it was the first time I wanted something beyond what I had been trained to want. I loved her, and it was the first time I loved someone beyond those I had been expected to love. Creating a life with her was the first original idea I'd ever had and the first decision I made as a free woman. After thirty years of contorting myself to fit inside someone else's idea of love, I finally had a love that fit—custom made for me, by me. I'd fi-

nally asked myself what I wanted instead of what the world
wanted from me. I felt alive. I'd tasted freedom, and I wanted
more.

I looked hard at my faith, my friendships, my work, my
sexuality, my entire life and asked: How much of this was my
idea? Do I truly want any of this, or is this what I was conditioned to want? Which of my beliefs are of my own creation
and which were programmed into me? How much of who I've
become is inherent, and how much was just inherited? How
much of the way I look and speak and behave is just how other
people have trained me to look and speak and behave? How
many of the things I've spent my life chasing are just dirty pink
bunnies? Who was I before I became who the world told me
to be?

Over time, I walked away from my cages. I slowly built a
new marriage, a new faith, a new worldview, a new purpose, a
new family, and a new identity by design instead of default.
From my imagination instead of my indoctrination. From my
wild instead of from my training.

What follows are stories about how I got caged—and how
I got free.

apples

I am ten years old, and I'm sitting in a small room in the back of Nativity Catholic Church with twenty other kids. I am at CCD, where my parents send me on Wednesday nights to learn about God. Our CCD teacher is my classmate's mom. I do not remember her name, but I do remember that she keeps telling us that she is an accountant during the day. Her family needed service hours, so she volunteered to work in the gift shop. Instead, the church assigned her to room 423, fifth-grade CCD. So now—on Wednesdays between 6:30 and 7:30 P.M.—she teaches children about God.

She asks us to sit on the carpet in front of her chair, because she is going to explain to us how God made people. I hurry to get a spot in front. I am very curious about how and why I was made. I notice that our teacher does not have a Bible or any other books in her lap. She is going to speak from memory. I am impressed.

She begins.

"God made Adam and put him in a beautiful garden. Adam was God's favorite creation, so He told Adam that his only jobs were to be happy, rule over the garden, and name the animals. Adam's life was almost perfect. Except that he got lonely and stressed. He wanted some company and help naming the animals. So he told God that he wanted a companion and a helper. One night, God helped Adam give birth to Eve. From inside Adam's body, a woman was born. That is why she is called woman. Because women came from the womb of man. Womb—man."

I am so amazed that I forget to raise my hand.

"Wait. Adam gave birth to *Eve*? But don't people come from women's bodies? Shouldn't boys be called woman? Shouldn't all people be called woman?"

My teacher says, "Raise your hand, Glennon."

I raise my hand. She motions for me to put it back down. The boy sitting to my left rolls his eyes at me.

Our teacher goes on.

"Adam and Eve were happy, and everything stayed perfect for a while.

"But then God said there was one tree they couldn't eat from: the Tree of Knowledge. Even though it was the only thing that Eve wasn't allowed to want, she wanted an apple from that tree anyway. So one day, she got hungry, picked the apple off the tree, and took a bite. Then she tricked Adam into taking a bite, too. As soon as Adam bit into the apple, Eve and Adam felt shame for the first time and tried to hide from God. But God sees everything, so God knew. God banished Adam and Eve from the garden. Then He cursed them and their future children, and for the first time, suffering existed on the earth. This is why we still suffer today, because Eve's original sin is inside of all of us. That sin is wanting to know more than we are supposed to know, wanting more instead of being grateful for what we have, and doing what we want to do instead of what we should do."

That was some careful accounting. I had no further questions.

blow jobs

My husband and I began working with a therapist after he admitted that he had been sleeping with other women. Now we save up our problems throughout the week and take them to her on Tuesday evenings. When friends ask me if she's any good, I say, "I guess so. I mean, we're still married."

Today I've asked to see her alone. I'm tired and jittery because I spent all night silently rehearsing how to tell her what I'm about to tell her.

I sit quietly in my chair, hands folded in my lap. She sits upright in the chair across from me. She wears a crisp white pantsuit, sensible heels, no makeup. A wooden bookshelf crowded with textbooks and framed degrees climbs the wall behind her like a bean stalk. Her pen is poised above a leather notebook in her lap, ready to pin me down in black and white. I remind myself: *Speak calmly and confidently, Glennon, like a grown-up.*

"I have something important to tell you. I've fallen in love. I am wildly in love. Her name is Abby."

My therapist's mouth falls open, just enough for me to notice it. She says nothing for an eternal moment. Then she breathes very deeply and says, "Okay."

She pauses, starts again. "Glennon, you know that whatever this is—it's not real. These feelings are *not real*. Whatever future you're imagining here: That's not real, either. This is nothing but a dangerous distraction. It won't end well. It has to stop."

I start to say, "You don't understand. This is different." But then I think about all the people who have sat in this chair and insisted: *This is different*.

If she won't let me have Abby, I need to make my case, at least, for never again having my husband.

"I cannot sleep with him again," I say. "You know how hard I've tried. Sometimes I think I've forgiven. But then he climbs on top of me, and I hate him again. It's been years and I don't want to be difficult, so I close my eyes and try to float away until it's over. But then I accidentally land back inside my body, and what I land in is white-hot fiery rage. It's like: I try to go dead inside but there is always a little life left in me, and that life makes sex unbearable. I can't be alive during sex, but I can't get dead enough, either, so there's no solution. I just—I don't want to do it anymore."

I am furious that tears come, but they do. I am begging now. Mercy, please.

Two women. One white suit. Six framed degrees. One open notebook. One pen, poised.

Then: "Glennon, have you tried just giving him blow jobs instead? Many women find blow jobs to be less intimate."

directions

I have a son and two daughters, until they tell me otherwise.

My children believe that the shower is a magical portal of ideas.

My youngest recently said to me, "Mom, it's like I don't have any ideas all day, but when I get in the shower my brain is full of cool stuff. I think it's the water or something."

"Could be the water," I said. "Or it could be that the shower's the only place you're not plugged in—so you can hear your own thoughts in there."

She looked at me and said, "Huh?"

"That thing that happens to you in the shower, babe. It's called *thinking*. It's something folks did before Google. Thinking is like . . . it's like googling your own brain."

"Oh," she said. "Cool."

That same child steals my expensive shampoo once a week, so the other day I stomped to the bathroom she shares with her teenage brother and sister to steal it back. I opened the shower curtain and noticed the twelve empty bottles littering the tub's edge. All the bottles on the right side were red, white, and blue. All the bottles on the left side were pink and purple.

I picked up a red bottle from what was clearly my son's side. It was tall, rectangular, bulky. It yelled at me in bold red, white, and blue letters:

3X BIGGER,

DOESN'T ROB YOU OF YOUR DIGNITY,

ARMOR UP IN MAN SCENT,

DROP-KICK DIRT, THEN SLAM ODOR WITH A FOLDING CHAIR.

I thought: *What the hell? Is my son taking a shower or preparing for war in here?*

I picked up one of the girls' slim, metallic, pink bottles. Instead of barking marching orders at me, that bottle, in cursive, flowy font, whispered disconnected adjectives: *alluring, radiant, gentle, pure, illuminating, enticing, touchable, light, creamy.* Not a verb to be found. Nothing to do here, just a list of things to be.

I looked around for a moment to ensure that the shower was not, in fact, a magic portal that had somehow transported me back in time. Nope. There I was, in the twenty-first century, when boys are still being taught that real men are big, bold, violent, invulnerable, disgusted by femininity, and responsible for conquering women and the world. When girls are still being taught that real women must be quiet, pretty, small, passive, and desirable so they'll be worthy of being conquered. Here we all are. Our sons and daughters are still being shamed out of their full humanity before they even get dressed in the morning.

Our children are too vast to fit themselves inside these rigid, mass-produced bottles. But they'll lose themselves trying.

polar bears

Several years ago, my daughter Tish's teacher called and said that there was a "situation" at school. During a discussion about wildlife, she'd mentioned to the class that polar bears were losing their homes and food sources because of the melting ice caps. She showed the students a photo of a dying polar bear as an example of the many effects of global warming.

The rest of the kindergarteners thought that this was sad information but not sad enough to keep them from, you know, soldiering on to recess. Not Tish. The teacher reported to me that when the lesson ended and the other kids popped off the carpet to run outside, Tish remained seated, alone, mouth wide open, stunned into paralysis, her little shocked face asking:

"WHAT? Did you just say the polar bears are *dying*? Because the *Earth is melting*? The same Earth that we live on? Did you just drop that little tidbit of terror *ON US AT CIRCLE TIME*?"

Tish eventually made it outside, but was unable to participate in recess that day. The other kids tried to get her off the bench to play four square with them, but she remained close to her teacher, wide-eyed, asking, "Do the grown-ups know about this? What are they going to do? Are other animals in trouble, too? Where is that hungry polar bear's mom?"

For the next month, our family's life revolved around polar bears. We bought polar bear posters and papered Tish's wall with them. "To remember, Mom—I've got to remember." We sponsored four polar bears online. We talked about polar bears at dinner, at breakfast, during car pool, and at parties. We discussed polar bears so incessantly, in fact, that after a few weeks I began to hate polar bears with every fiber of my being. I began to rue the day that polar bears were ever born. I tried everything I could think of to yank Tish out of her polar bear abyss. I coddled her, I snapped at her, and finally I just lied to her.

I asked a friend to send me an "official" email pretending to be the "Ambassador of the Arctic," announcing that, once and for all, the ice caps were fixed and all the polar bears were suddenly A-OK. I opened that fraudulent email and called to Tish in her room, "Oh my gosh, baby! Come here! Look what I just got! Good news!" Tish read the email silently, then turned slowly toward me with a scathing look of scorn. She knew the email was fake because she is sensitive, not stupid. The polar bear saga continued, full force.

One night I tucked Tish into bed and was tiptoeing out of her room with the joy of a mother who is almost to the promised land. (Everybody's asleep and I've got my couch and carbs and Netflix and no one is allowed to touch me or talk to me until the sun rises, hallelujah.) I was closing the door behind me when Tish whispered, "Wait. Mom?"

Damnit to hell.

"What, honey?"

"It's the polar bears."

OH, HELLLL NO.

I walked back to her bed and stared down at her, a little maniacally. Tish looked up at me and said, "Mommy. I just can't stop thinking: It's the polar bears now. But nobody cares. So next, it's gonna be us."

Then she rolled over, fell asleep, and left me all alone in the dark room, stunned into paralysis myself. I stood over her, eyes wide, arms wrapped around my body. "Oh. My. God. The polllaaarrr bears!! We have to save the mother freaking polar bears! Next it's gonna be us. What is *wrong* with us??"

Then I looked down at my baby and thought: *Ah. You are not crazy to be heartbroken over the polar bears; the rest of us are crazy not to be.*

Tish couldn't go to recess because she was paying attention to what her teacher said. As soon as she heard the polar bear news, she let herself feel the horror and know the wrongness and imagine the inevitable outcome. Tish is sensitive, and that is her superpower. The opposite of sensitive is not brave. It's not brave to refuse to pay attention, to refuse to notice, to refuse to feel and know and imagine. The opposite of sensitive is insensitive, and that's no badge of honor.

Tish senses. Even as the world tries to speed by her, she is slowly taking it in. *Wait, stop. That thing you said about the polar bears . . . it made me feel something and wonder something. Can we stay there for a moment? I have feelings. I have questions. I'm not ready to run outside to recess yet.*

In most cultures, folks like Tish are identified early, set apart as shamans, medicine people, poets, and clergy. They are considered eccentric but critical to the survival of the group because they are able to hear things others don't hear and see things others don't see and feel things others don't feel. The culture depends on the sensitivity of a few, because nothing can be healed if it's not sensed first.

But our society is so hell-bent on expansion, power, and efficiency at all costs that the folks like Tish—like me—are inconvenient. We slow the world down. We're on the bow of the *Titanic*, pointing, crying out, "Iceberg! Iceberg!" while everyone else is below deck, yelling back, "We just want to keep dancing!" It is easier to call us broken and dismiss us than to consider that we are responding appropriately to a broken world.

My little girl is not broken. She is a prophet. I want to be wise enough to stop with her, ask her what she feels, and listen to what she knows.

tick marks

It's my senior year of high school, and I still haven't been nominated to Homecoming Court.

Homecoming Court is made up of the ten most popular students in each grade. Those ten will dress up and ride in convertibles in the homecoming parade, dress up and walk the field at halftime, dress up and walk the halls wearing their Homecoming Court sashes. Homecoming is High School Fashion Week, and the rest of us will watch the members of the Court walk the runways from our places in the shadows.

Our teachers pass out ballots in English class and instruct us to vote for the students who should ascend to court. Each year we vote en masse for the same ten Golden Ones. We all know who they are. It feels like we were born knowing who they are. The Golden Ones stand together in a closed circle—like the sun—in the hallways, at football games, at the mall, and in our minds. We are not supposed to look directly at them, which is difficult because they have shiny hair and their bodies are alluring, light, and radiant. None of them is a bully. Bullying would require paying far too much attention and exerting far too much effort. They are above and beyond that. Their job is to ignore the rest of us, and our job is to judge ourselves against the standards they set. Our existence makes them Golden, and their existence makes us miserable. Yet we vote for them year after year, because the rules control us even at the privacy of our own desks. *Vote for the Golden Ones. They have followed directions perfectly, they are what we are all supposed to be, so they should win. Fair is fair.*

I am not Golden, but the Golden Ones' light reflects on me just often enough that I am tinged. They invite me to their parties occasionally and I go, but when I get there they don't talk to me much. I assume I'm there because they need some ungold around in order to feel their goldenness. Goldenness requires *contrast*. So when they stand in circles at football games, they let me join their circle, but they don't talk to me there, either. I feel terribly uncomfortable, left out, and ridiculous in those circles. I remind myself that what is really happening in the circle doesn't matter. What matters is what people outside the circle perceive to be happening there. What matters is not what is real, but what I can convince *others* is real. What matters is not how I feel inside, but how I appear to feel on the outside. How I *appear to feel* will determine how others feel about me. What matters is how others feel about me. So I act like someone who feels Golden.

By mid-September, the buzz of homecoming preparations has reached fever pitch. We've just cast our ballots, and the winners will be announced in sixth period. I'm in student government class, and our job is to count the votes. My friend Lisa is pulling ballots out of a box one at a time and reading the names aloud while I tally the votes. She calls out the same names again and again: Tina. Kelly. Jessa. Tina. Kelly Jessa

Susan. Jessa. Susan Tina Tina Tina. And then Glennon. A couple more . . . Glennon. Glennon. Lisa looks at me, raises her eyebrows, and smiles. I roll my eyes and look away, but my heart pounds in my chest. *Holy shit. They think I'm Golden.* I can see that the ballot box is almost empty, but the votes are close and I could make it. I could make it. I need just two more votes. I look over at Lisa, and her eyes are diverted. With my pencil I make two more marks next to my name. Tick. Tick. Lisa and I count the votes. I have been nominated for Homecoming Court.

I am now a girl who, even when she's forty-four years old, can roll her eyes and mention, offhandedly, well, I was on the Homecoming Court. Others will roll their eyes, too (high school!), but they will also register: Ah. You were Golden. Golden is decided early, and it sticks, somehow, even when we are grown and know so much better, so much more. Once Golden, always Golden.

For more than a decade I have written and spoken openly about addiction, sex, infidelity, and depression. Shamelessness is my spiritual practice. Yet I have never admitted to committing high school voter fraud to anyone but my wife. When I told her that I'd finally written this story, she winced and asked, "Are you sure, babe? Are you sure you should tell that one?"

I think what makes this story unforgivable is the desperation. It's the wanting—the caring so much. If one cannot be Golden, then one must pretend that one does not want to be. It's so uncool, so terribly uncool, to want to belong so badly that you're willing to cheat for it. But I did.

I rigged an election trying to be Golden. I spent sixteen years with my head in a toilet trying to be light. I drank myself numb for a decade, trying to be pleasant. I've giggled at and slept with assholes, trying to be touchable. I've held my tongue so hard I tasted blood, trying to be gentle. I've spent thousands on potions and poisons, trying to be youthful. I have denied myself for decades, trying to be pure.

algorithms

Several months after I found out my husband had repeatedly been unfaithful, I still didn't know whether I'd stay or go. I didn't even know if the new throw pillow on my couch would stay or go. I was a terribly indecisive woman. When I told the counselor at my kids' school how uncertain I felt, she said, "It's not hard decisions that mess up kids, it's indecision. Your kids need to know which way this is going to go."

I said, "Well, they can't know until I know."

She said, "You need to figure out *how to know.*"

Back then, the only way I knew *how to know* was to poll and research. I began polling. I called each of my friends, hoping that they would know what I should do. Next I began my research. I read every article I could find about infidelity, divorce, and children, hoping the experts would know what I should do. My polling and research results were maddeningly inconclusive.

Finally, I turned to the World Wide Web to see if an invisible conglomeration of strangers, trolls, and bots knew what I should do with my one wild and precious life. That is how I found myself in bed at 3:00 A.M., shoveling Ben & Jerry's into my mouth, typing into my Google search bar:

What should I do if my husband is a cheater but also an amazing dad?

gatherings

My seventeen-year-old son, Chase, and his friends are in the family room watching a movie. I've been trying to leave them alone, but it's hard for me. I understand that most teenagers think their moms are uncool, but I am certain I'm the exception.

I stand at the door and peek inside. The boys are draped all over the couch. The girls have arranged themselves in tiny, tidy roly-poly piles on the floor. My young daughters are perched at the feet of the older girls, quietly worshipping.

My son looks over at me and half smiles. "Hi, Mom."

I need an excuse to be there, so I ask, "Anybody hungry?"

What comes next seems to unfold in slow motion.

Every single boy keeps his eyes on the TV and says, "YES!"

The girls are silent at first. Then each girl diverts her eyes from the television screen and scans the faces of the other girls. Each looks to *a friend's face* to discover if *she herself is hungry*. Some kind of telepathy is happening among them. They are polling. They are researching. They are gathering consensus, permission, or denial.

Somehow the collective silently appoints a French-braided, freckle-nosed spokesgirl.

She looks away from the faces of her friends and over at me. She smiles politely and says, "We're fine, thank you."

The boys looked inside themselves. The girls looked outside themselves.

We forgot how to know when we learned how to please.

This is why we live hungry.

rules

My friend Ashley took her first hot yoga class recently. She walked into the room, unrolled her mat, sat down, and waited for something to happen.

"It was exceptionally hot in there," she told me.

When the instructor—young and confident—finally walked into the room, Ashley was already dripping with sweat. The instructor announced, "We'll start soon. You are going to get very hot, but you can't leave this room. No matter how you begin to feel, stay strong. Don't leave. This is the work."

The class got started, and a few minutes in, the walls began to close in on Ashley. She felt light-headed and sick. Each breath became harder and harder to come by. Twice her vision became spotty, then briefly went black. She looked at the door and felt desperate to run toward it. She spent ninety minutes terrified, close to hyperventilating, holding back tears. But she did not leave that room.

The moment the instructor ended the class and opened the door, Ashley jumped off her mat and ran into the hallway. She kept her hand over her mouth until she found the bathroom. She threw the door open and vomited all over the sink, the wall, the floor.

While she was on her hands and knees wiping up her own puke with paper towels, she thought: *What is wrong with me? Why did I stay and suffer? The door wasn't even locked.*

dragons

When I was a little girl, my godmother gave me a snow globe as a birthday gift. It was small and round, like a palm-sized crystal ball. In its center stood a red dragon with sparkly scales, bright green eyes, and fiery wings. When I first took it home, I put it on the nightstand beside my bed. Then I'd lie awake at night, wide-eyed, feeling afraid that the dragon existed so close to me in the dark. So one night I climbed out of bed and moved the snow globe to the highest shelf in my room.

Every once in a while, only in the light of day, I'd pull my desk chair over, climb up, and pull the snow globe off the shelf. I'd shake it, get still, and watch the snowflakes swirl. As they began to settle, the fiery red dragon in the center of the globe would emerge, and I'd feel a chilly thrill. That dragon was magical and scary, always there, unmoving, just waiting.

My friend Megan is five years sober now after a decade of alcohol and drug abuse. Lately, she's been trying to figure out what happened to her—how addiction had taken over the life of such a strong woman.

On Megan's wedding day, she sat in the back of the chapel knowing she didn't want to marry the man waiting for her at the end of the aisle. She knew it from her roots.

She married him anyway, because she was thirty-five years old and getting married was what she was supposed to do. She married him anyway, because there were so many people she would have disappointed if she had called it off. There was only one of her, so she disappointed herself instead. She said "I do" while her insides said "I don't," and then she spent the next decade trying not to know what she knew: that she had betrayed herself and that her life would not really begin until she stopped betraying herself. The only way not to know was to get wasted and stay that way, so she started drinking heavily during her honeymoon. The drunker she became, the more distance she felt from the dragon inside her. After a while, the booze and drugs became her problem, which was convenient because she didn't have to deal with her real problem anymore.

We're like snow globes: We spend all of our time, energy, words, and money creating a flurry, trying not to know, making sure that the snow doesn't settle so we never have to face the fiery truth inside us—solid and unmoving.

The relationship is over. The wine is winning. The pills aren't for back pain anymore. He's never coming back. That book won't write itself. The move is the only way. Quitting this job will save my life. It is abuse. You never grieved him. It's been six months since we made love. Spending a lifetime hating her is no life at all.

We keep ourselves shaken up because there are dragons in our center.

One night, back when my children were babies, I was reading a book of poetry in the bathtub. I came across a poem called "A Secret Life" about deep secrets and how we all have them. I thought: *Well, I haven't had one since I got sober. I don't keep secrets anymore.* That felt good. But then I read:

> *It becomes what you'd most protect*
> *if the government said you can protect*
> *one thing, all else is ours. . . .*
> *it's what*
> *radiates and what can hurt*
> *if you get too close to it.*

I stopped reading and thought: *Oh, wait.*

There's one thing.

One thing I haven't even told my sister.

My secret that radiates is that I find women infinitely more compelling and attractive than men. My secret is my suspicion that I was made to make love to a woman and cuddle with a woman and rely on a woman and live and die with a woman.

Then I thought: *So odd. That cannot be real. You've got a husband and three children. Your life is more than good enough.*

As I climbed out of the tub and shook my hair dry, I told myself: *Maybe in a different life.*

Isn't that interesting?

As if I had more than one.

arms

I sit in a cold plastic seat near the airport gate, stare at my suitcase, sip airport coffee. It's bitter and weak. I look at the plane through the gate window. How many of those will I board in the coming year? A hundred? I'm bitter and weak, too.

If I board, this plane will take me to Chicago O'Hare, where I'll search for a driver holding a sign with my (husband's) last name on it. I'll raise my hand and watch the driver's face register surprise that I am a small woman in sweatpants instead of a large man in a suit. The driver will deliver me to the Palmer Hotel—where a national book conference is being held. There I'll stand on a stage in a grand ballroom and speak to a few hundred librarians about my soon-to-be-released memoir, *Love Warrior*.

Love Warrior—the story of the dramatic destruction and painstaking reconstruction of my family—is expected to be one of the biggest books of the year. I will be promoting it on stages and in the media for, well, forever.

I am trying to find my feelings about this. Fear? Excitement? Shame? I can't isolate anything specific. I stare at the plane, wondering how to explain my life's most intimate, complicated experience to a sea of strangers within my seven allotted minutes. I have written a book, and now I must become a commercial for the book I have written. What is the point of being a writer if I have to say words about the words I've already written? Do painters have to draw about their paintings?

I'd been at this airport gate starting line before. Three years before, I'd released my first book and traveled the country telling the story of how I'd finally found happily-ever-after by trading my lifelong food and booze addictions for a son, a husband, and writing. I'd stood on stages all over the country and repeated the book's message to hopeful women: *Carry on. Life is hard, but you are a warrior. One day it will all come together for you, too.*

Right after that first book's ink dried, I sat in a therapist's office and listened to my husband say that he'd been sleeping around since our wedding.

I held my breath as he said, "There have been other women," and when I inhaled again, the air was made of smelling salts. He kept apologizing while looking down at his hands, and the impotent stammering made me laugh out loud. My laughter made both men—my husband and his therapist—visibly uncomfortable. Their discomfort made me feel powerful. I looked at the door and willed adrenaline to carry me out of that building, across the parking lot, and into my minivan.

I sat in the driver's seat for a while and realized that the revelation of my husband's betrayal did not leave me feeling the despair of a wife with a broken heart. I was feeling the rage of a writer with a broken plot. Hell hath no fury like a memoirist whose husband just fucked up her story.

I was furious with him and disgusted with myself. I'd let down my guard and trusted that the other characters in my story would act as they should and that my plot would unfold as I'd mapped it. I'd rendered my own future and my children vulnerable by ceding creative control to another character. What an idiot. Never again. I would take back full control, starting now. This was my story and my family, and I would decide how it ended. I'd take this shit I'd been handed, and I'd spin it into gold.

I took control back with words, sentences, chapters, and scripts. I started with the story's resolution in mind—a healed, whole family—and worked backward from there. There would be rage, pain, therapy, self-discovery, forgiveness, reluctant trust, then eventually: fresh intimacy and redemption. I do not know if I lived the next few years and then wrote about what happened or if I wrote the next few years and then made it all happen. It didn't matter. What mattered was that at the end of that blur of time I had myself a dark love story—a drama of betrayal and forgiveness, pain and redemption, brokenness and healing. In book form and family form. Checkmate, Life.

In Ann Patchett's *Truth & Beauty,* a reader approaches Lucy at her book-signing table and asks of her memoir, "How do you remember all of that?"

"I don't remember it," she says. "I *write* it."

When *Love Warrior* was complete, I handed the manuscript to Craig and said, "Here. Here is what it all meant. I made it all mean something. We won the war. Our family made it. We are a love story after all. You are welcome."

Now the war has ended, and I want to go home. But home is still a foxhole with me and Craig left staring at each other, wondering: What now? What did we win?

I call my sister and ask if I can cancel the book launch event in Chicago. I want her to tell me that this will be fine, no big deal. She says, "We can cancel, but it will be a big deal. You committed to this."

So I do this thing I do. From the outside I imagine it looks like a straightening, a stiffening. From the inside it feels like turning my liquid self to a solid. Water to ice. *Glennon has left the building.* I've got this. I board the plane to go tell a story I'm not sure I believe.

It will be okay. I'll just tell it like a story instead of a life. As if I am past the end instead of stuck in the middle. I'll tell the truth, but I'll tell it with a slant: I'll blame myself just enough; present him in the most sympathetic light; attach my bulimia to my frigidity and my frigidity to his infidelity. I'll tell how the cheating led to my self-reflection, how self-reflection led to forgiveness and pain led to redemption. I'll tell it so that people will decide: *Of course. It was leading to this ending all along. I see. It all had to happen exactly that way.* That is what I will decide, too.

The moral arc of our life bends toward meaning—especially if we bend it that way with all our damn might.

I arrive in Chicago and meet my book publicist at the Palmer House hotel, where the event is being held. This weekend is the literary Super Bowl, and she's buzzing. We are on our way to a dinner where ten authors will get to know one another before we head into the ballroom and pitch our upcoming books from the stage. This dinner, which I have just learned about a few hours before, has heightened my introvert terror alert level from yellow to red.

The room where the authors are to have dinner is small, with two long conference tables pushed together to form a square. Instead of sitting, people are milling. Milling with people I do not know is my idea of hell on Earth. I do not mill. I walk over to the drink table and pour an ice water. A famous writer walks over and introduces herself. She asks, "Are you Glennon? I've been wanting to talk to you. You're the Christian one, right?"

Yes, I'm the one.

"My new book is about a woman who has a religious experience and becomes a Christian. Do you believe it? A Christian! It feels so real to her! I don't know how my readers will react: Will people be able to take her seriously? What do you think? Do you feel like people take you seriously?"

I say the most serious thing I can think of and then excuse myself.

I look at the table. No assigned seats, damnit. George Saunders sits quietly at the end of the table. He seems gentle and kind and I'd like to sit next to him, but he is a man and I don't know how to talk to men. At the end of the table is a young woman with calm energy. I sit down next to her. She is a twenty-something releasing her first children's book. I ask her question after question while considering how wonderful it would be if the organizers would just place our books on the table, so we could get to know each other by reading silently. We butter our rolls. Salads are served. As I'm reaching for dressing, the children's book lady looks over at the door. I look over, too.

Suddenly, a woman is standing where nothingness used to be. She takes up the entire doorway, the entire room, the entire universe. She has short hair, platinum on top, shaved on the sides. She is wearing a long trench coat, a red scarf, a warm half smile, cool steel confidence. She stands still there for a moment, taking inventory of the room. I stare at her and take inventory of my entire life.

My whole being says:
There She Is.

Then, I lose control of my body. I stand up and open my arms wide.

She looks over, cocks her head to the side, raises her eyebrows, smiles at me.

Fuck Fuck Fuck Why am I standing? Why are my arms open? Oh my God, What Am I Doing?

I sit back down.

She walks around the table and shakes hands with everyone. When she gets to me, I stand up again, turn around, face her. "I'm Abby," she says.

I ask if I can hug her, because what if this is my only chance? She smiles and opens her arms. Then—the smell that will become home to me—skin like powder and fabric softener blended with the wool of her coat and her cologne and something that smelled like air, like outdoors, like crisp sky, like a baby and a woman and a man and the whole world.

The only seat left is at the far end of the table, so she walks away from me and sits down. She'll later tell me that she didn't eat or speak because all of her energy was spent trying not to stare. Mine, too.

Dinner ends, and there is more milling. Oh my God, more milling and now with a revolution in the room. I excuse myself to go to the bathroom and kill two milling minutes. When I walk out, she is standing in the hallway, watching the bathroom door, waiting. She motions to me to come over. I look behind me to make sure it's me she's talking to. She laughs. She *laughs*.

Then it's time to walk to the ballroom. We separate ourselves from the pack somehow. There are people three feet in front of us and behind us, but here we are, walking alone, together. I want so badly to be interesting. But she is so cool, and I don't know how to be cool. I've not been cool a day in my life. I am warm—burning up—sweating through my shirt already.

She starts talking, thank God. She tells me about the book she's about to release. She says, "But things are hard right now. You've probably heard."

"Heard what? I have not heard. What would I have heard, and where would I have heard it?"

She says, "The news, maybe? ESPN?"

"Um, no, I have not heard the news on ESPN," I say.

She speaks, slowly at first, then all at once.

"I'm a soccer player. *Was* a soccer player. I just retired, and I'm not sure what I am now. I got a DUI last month. It was all over the news. I watched my mug shot scroll across the ticker for days. I can't believe I did it. I've been really lost and depressed the last couple of years, and I just . . . I screwed up. I've always been about honor, and I ruined my whole legacy. I let everybody down. I hurt the whole team, maybe. And now they want me to write my book as some kind of hero athlete puff piece, but I keep thinking: What if I'm just honest? What if I write the truth about my life?"

I am sad for her, but I am thrilled for me. In our four minutes together she has asked me about the three subjects I know best: drinking, writing, and shame. *This is my jam.* I've got this. Hot damn.

I put my hand on her arm. Electrical currents. I pull back and recover enough to say, "Listen, I have a rap sheet as long as your arm. I'd write it all. I'd be honest. I don't know much about the sports world, but I do know that out here in the real world, we like real people."

She stops walking, so I do, too. She turns and looks directly at me. It appears that she's about to say something. I hold my breath. Then she turns and keeps walking. I start breathing and walking, too. We enter the ballroom and follow the other authors through a sea of round tables, white tablecloths, thirty-foot ceilings, crystal chandeliers. We end up at the dais, climb the stairs, and see that we've been seated next to each other. We walk toward our places, and when we arrive, she puts her hand on the back of my chair. She cannot decide whether to pull it out for me. She does. "Thank you," I say.

We sit down, and the writer seated next to Abby asks where she's from.

"We live in Portland," Abby answers.

The writer says, "Oh, I love Portland."

Abby says, "Yeah."

Something about the way she says "Yeah" makes me listen very, very hard.

"I don't know how much longer I'll be there. We moved there because we thought it would be a good place to raise a family."

I can tell, just by the way she says this, that there is no *we* left. I want to save her from follow-up questions, so I say, "Oh, people like us can't live in Portland. We're Portland on the inside. We need sunshine on the outside."

I am immediately embarrassed by what I've just said. *Portland on the inside?* What the hell do those words even mean? *People like us?* Why did I say us? *Us?* How terribly presumptuous to suggest the concept of us. Us.

Us. Us. Us.

She looks at me, her eyes widen, and she smiles. I change my mind. I don't know what I meant, but I'm glad I said it. I decide that heaven is saying anything that makes this woman smile like that.

The event begins. When it is my turn to walk to the podium and speak, I disregard half of my planned speech and say things about shame and freedom that I want Abby to hear. I look at the hundreds of people in front of me and think only of her behind me. When I finish, I sit down and Abby looks at me. Her eyes are red.

The dinner ends, and people begin to approach our table. A line forms in front of Abby fifty people deep. She turns and asks me to sign a copy of my book for her. I do. Then she turns back toward the crowd and starts smiling, signing, making small talk. She is comfortable, confident, gracious. She is used to this.

A curly-haired woman who had walked into dinner behind Abby approaches our table. I can tell she is waiting to talk to me. I smile and motion her over. She leans in to me, as close as possible, and whispers, "I'm sorry. I've never done anything like this before. I just, I know Abby really well, like a sister. I don't know what happened here in the last hour, but I've never seen her like this. I just, I really feel like she needs you in her life. Somehow. This is so weird. I'm sorry." This woman is flustered, and she has tears in her eyes. She hands me her business card. I understand that my answer will be important to her.

I say, "Okay. Yes. Yes, of course."

My friend Dynna from my publishing house is waiting so that we can walk out together. I look over at Abby, still forty fans left to sign for.

I am not sad to leave Abby. I am excited to leave her so I can think about her. I am excited to leave because I realize I have never in my life felt this alive, and now I just want to go out into the world and walk around feeling this alive. I just want to start being this new person I have just suddenly, somehow become.

I say, "Bye Abby." Oh my God, I've said her name. *Abby.* I wonder if it's okay or if I should have asked permission to use this word that sends shock waves rippling through me. She turns toward me, smiles, waves. She looks *expectant*. Her face is asking a question that one day I'll answer.

Dynna and I walk out of the ballroom and into a grand hallway. She stops me and asks, "How do you think it went?"

I say, "It was amazing."

Dynna says, "I agree. You were on fire up there. Different somehow."

"Oh, you meant the speech. I was talking about the whole night. I felt the oddest thing. I felt like Abby and I had some kind of connection."

Dynna grabbed my arm and said, "I cannot believe you just said that. I can't believe this. I swear to God, I felt it, too. I felt something happening between you from all the way in the back of the ballroom. This is so wild."

I stared at her and said, "It was. It is. This whole night . . . the connection between us . . . it was just like . . ."

Dynna looked hard at me and then said, "Like you two would have been together in another life?"

Part Two

Keys

DROPPING KEYS

The small woman
Builds cages for everyone
She
Knows.
While the sage,
Who has to duck her head
When the moon is low,
Keeps dropping keys all night long
For the
Beautiful
Rowdy
Prisoners.
  —HAFIZ

I was never completely gone. My spark was always inside me, smoldering. But I sure as hell felt gone for a long while. My childhood bulimia morphed into alcoholism and drug use, and I stayed numb for sixteen years. Then, when I was twenty-six I got pregnant and sober. Sobriety was the field in which I began to remember my wild.

It went like this: I began building the kind of life a woman is supposed to build. I became a good wife, mother, daughter, Christian, citizen, writer, woman. But while I made school lunches, wrote memoirs, rushed through airports, made small talk with neighbors, carried on with my outer life, I felt an electric restlessness buzzing inside me. It was like constant thunder rolling *right there* beneath my skin—a thunder made of joy and pain and rage and longing and love too deep, scalding, and tender for this world. It felt like hot water simmering, always threatening to boil.

I was afraid of what was inside me. It felt powerful enough to destroy every bit of the lovely life I'd built. Like how I never feel safe on a balcony because: *What if I jump?*

It's okay, I told myself. I'll keep myself and my people safe by keeping my insides hidden.

I was amazed at how easy this was. I was filled with electric thunder, simmering water, fiery red and gold, but all I had to do was smile and nod and the world would take me for easy breezy blue. Sometimes I wondered if I wasn't the only one using her skin to contain herself. Maybe we are all fire wrapped in skin, trying to look cool.

My boiling point was the moment Abby stepped through that doorway. I looked at her, and I could no longer contain myself. I lost control. Fire-red and golden rolling bubbles of pain and love and longing filled me, brought me to my feet, threw my arms open wide, insisting: *There. She. Is.*

For a long while I thought that what happened that day was some kind of fairy-tale magic. I thought the words *There She Is* came to me from on high. Now I know that *There She Is* came from within. That wild rowdiness that had simmered for so long and then turned itself into words and lifted me was *me*. The voice I finally heard that day was my own—the girl I'd locked away at ten years old, the girl I was before the world told me who to be—and she said: *Here I Am. I'm taking over now.*

When I was a child, I felt what I needed to feel and I followed my gut and I planned only from my imagination. I was wild until I was tamed by shame. Until I started hiding and numbing my feelings for fear of being too much. Until I started deferring to others' advice instead of trusting my own intuition. Until I became convinced that my imagination was ridiculous and my desires were selfish. Until I surrendered myself to the cages of others' expectations, cultural mandates, and institutional allegiances. Until I buried who I was in order to become what I should be. I lost myself when I learned how to please.

Sobriety was my painstaking resurrection. It was my return to wild. It was one long remembering. It was realizing that the hot electric thunder I felt buzzing and rolling inside was *me*— trying to get my attention, begging me to remember, insisting: *I'm still in here.*

So I finally unlocked and unleashed her. I set free my beautiful, rowdy, true wild self. I was right about her power. It was too big for the life I was living, so I systematically dismantled every piece of it.

Then I built a life of my own.

I did it by resurrecting the very parts of myself I was trained to mistrust, hide, and abandon in order to keep others comfortable:

My emotions

My intuition

My imagination

My courage

Those are the keys to freedom.

Those are *who we are*.

Will we be brave enough to unlock ourselves?

Will we be brave enough to set ourselves free?

Will we finally step out of our cages and say to ourselves, to our people, and to the world: *Here I Am*.

Feel

Key One: Feel It All

On my sixth day of sobriety, I went to my fifth recovery meeting. I sat in a cold plastic seat, trembling, trying to keep the coffee from spilling out of my paper cup and my feelings from spilling out of my skin. For sixteen years I had made damn sure that nothing touched me, and suddenly everything in the world was touching me. I was an exposed nerve. Everything hurt.

I was embarrassed to tell anyone how much I hurt, but I decided to try to explain it to the people in that circle. They were the first people I trusted with all of me, because they were the first people I ever heard tell the whole truth. They had shown me their insides so I showed them mine. I said something like "I'm Glennon, and I've been sober for six days. I feel awful. I think this awfulness is why I started drinking in the first place. I'm starting to worry that what was wrong with me wasn't the booze; it was underneath it. It was me. It doesn't seem like being alive is as hard for other people as it is for me. It just feels like there's some kind of secret to life I don't know. Like I'm doing it all wrong. Thanks for listening."

After the meeting ended, a woman walked over and sat down next to me. She said, "Thanks for sharing. I relate. I just wanted to tell you something that somebody told me in the beginning. It's okay to feel all of the stuff you're feeling. You're just becoming human again. You're not doing life wrong; you're doing it right. If there's any secret you're missing, it's that doing it right is just really hard. Feeling all your feelings is hard, but that's what they're for. Feelings are for feeling. All of them. Even the hard ones. The secret is that you're doing it right, and that doing it right hurts sometimes."

I did not know, before that woman told me, that all feelings were for feeling. I did not know that I was supposed to feel *everything*. I thought I was supposed to feel *happy*. I thought that happy was for feeling and that pain was for fixing and numbing and deflecting and hiding and ignoring. I thought that when life got hard, it was because I had gone wrong somewhere. I thought that pain was weakness and that I was supposed to *suck it up*. But the thing was that the more I sucked it up, the more food and booze I had to suck down.

That day, I began returning to myself—fearful and trembling, pregnant and six days sober, in a church basement with shitty fluorescent lights and terrible coffee—when a kind woman revealed to me that being fully human is not about feeling happy, it's about feeling everything. From that day forward, I began to practice feeling it all. I began to insist upon my right and responsibility to feel it all, even when taking the time and energy for feeling made me a little less efficient, a little less convenient, a little less pleasant.

In the past eighteen years, I have learned two things about pain.

First: I can feel everything and survive.

What I thought would kill me, didn't. Every time I said to myself: *I can't take this anymore*—I was wrong. The truth was that I could and did take it all—and I kept surviving. Surviving again and again made me less afraid of myself, of other people, of life. I learned that I'd never be free from pain but I could be free from the fear of pain, and that was enough. I finally stopped avoiding fires long enough to let myself burn, and what I learned was that I am like that burning bush: The fire of pain won't consume me. I can burn and burn and live. I can live on fire. I am fireproof.

Second: I can use pain to become.

I am here to keep becoming truer, more beautiful versions of myself again and again forever. To be alive is to be in a perpetual state of revolution. Whether I like it or not, pain is the fuel of revolution. Everything I need to become the woman I'm meant to be next is inside my feelings of now. Life is alchemy, and emotions are the fire that turns me to gold. I will continue to become only if I resist extinguishing myself a million times a day. If I can sit in the fire of my own feelings, I will keep becoming.

Consumer culture promises us that we can buy our way out of pain—that the reason we're sad and angry is not that being human hurts; it's because we don't have those countertops, her thighs, these jeans. This is a clever way to run an economy, but it is no way to run a life. Consuming keeps us distracted, busy, and numb. Numbness keeps us from becoming.

This is why every great spiritual teacher tells us the same story about humanity and pain: Don't avoid it. You need it to evolve, to become. And you are here to become.

Like Buddha, who had to leave his life of comfort to experience all kinds of human suffering before finding enlightenment.

Like Moses, who wandered forty years in the desert before seeing the promised land.

Like Westley from *The Princess Bride,* who said, "Life is pain, Highness. Anyone who says differently is selling something."

Like Jesus, who walked straight toward his own crucifixion.

First the pain, then the waiting, then the rising. All of our suffering comes when we try to get to our resurrection without allowing ourselves to be crucified first.

There is no glory except straight through your story.

Pain is not tragic. Pain is magic. Suffering is tragic. Suffering is what happens when we avoid pain and consequently miss our becoming. That is what I can and must avoid: missing my own evolution because I am too afraid to surrender to the process. Having such little faith in myself that I numb or hide or consume my way out of my fiery feelings again and again. So my goal is to stop abandoning myself—and stay. To trust that I'm strong enough to handle the pain that is necessary to the process of becoming. Because what scares me a hell of a lot more than pain is living my entire life and missing my becoming. What scares me more than feeling it all is missing it all.

These days, when pain comes, there are two of me.

There is the me that is miserable and afraid, and there is the me that is curious and excited. That second me is not a masochist, she's wise. She remembers. She remembers that even though I can't know what will come next in my life, I always know what comes next in the process. I know that when the pain and the waiting are here, the rising is on its way. I hope the pain will pass soon, but I'll wait it out because I've tested pain enough to trust it. And because who I will become tomorrow is so unforeseeable and specific that I'll need every bit of today's lessons to become her.

I keep a note stuck to my bathroom mirror:
Feel It All.

It reminds me that although I began to come back to life eighteen years ago, I resurrect myself every day, in every moment that I allow myself to feel and become. It's my daily reminder to let myself burn to ashes and rise, new.

Know

Key Two: Be Still and Know

Several years ago, very early one morning, I found myself unable to sleep again. It was 3:00 A.M., and I was wild-eyed, shaky, flailing, grasping for answers like a drowning woman desperate for air. I had just typed these words into my Google search window:

> What should I do if my husband is a cheater but also an
> amazing dad?

I stared at that question and thought: *Well. I have hit some sort of new rock bottom. I've just asked the* internet *to make the most important and personal decision of my life. Why do I trust everyone else on Earth more than I trust myself? WHERE THE HELL IS MY SELF? When did I lose touch with her?*

I clicked on article after article anyway. Distressingly, everyone thought I should do something different. The religious experts insisted that a good Christian would stay. Feminists argued that a strong woman would leave. Parenting articles preached that a good mother thinks only of what is best for her children. All of those differing opinions meant that I quite literally could not please everyone. That was a relief. When a woman finally learns that pleasing the world is impossible, she becomes free to learn how to please herself.

I looked at all of those contradictory opinions and thought: *If there is, in fact, an objective right or wrong way to handle this, why do all of these people have such different ideas about what a person should do?* I had an epiphany: It must be that *should* and *shouldn't, right* and *wrong, good* and *bad*—they're not wild. They're not real. They're just culturally constructed, artificial, ever-changing cages created to maintain institutions. It struck me that in every family, culture, or religion, ideas of right and wrong are the hot cattle prods, the barking sheepdogs that keep the masses in the herd. They are the bars that keep us caged.

I decided that if I kept doing the "right" thing, I would spend my life following someone else's directions instead of my own. I didn't want to live my life without living my life. I wanted to make my own decision as a free woman, from my soul, not my training. But the problem was, I didn't know how.

A few weeks later, I opened a card from a friend that said, in bold, capital, thick black lettering:

BE STILL AND KNOW.

I'd read that verse many times before, but it struck me freshly this time. It didn't say "Poll your friends and know" or "Read books by experts and know" or "Scour the internet and know." It suggested a different approach to knowing: *Just. Stop.*

StopMovingStopTalkingStopSearchingStopPanicking-
StopFlailing.

If you just stop doing, you'll start knowing.

This seemed like magical nonsense, but desperate women take desperate measures. I decided to experiment. After the kids left for school, I shut myself in my closet, sat down on a towel, closed my eyes, and did nothing but breathe. At first, each ten-minute session felt ten hours long. I checked my phone every few moments, planned my grocery lists, and mentally redecorated my living room. The only things I seemed to "know" on that floor were that I was hungry and itchy and suddenly desperate to fold laundry and reorganize my pantry. I was an input junkie thrown into detox. I was tempted to quit every second, but I was stern with myself: *Ten minutes a day is not too long to spend finding yourself, Glennon. For God's sake, you spend eighty minutes a day finding your keys.*

After a few weeks, like a gymnast who is able to stretch deeper after each training, I began to feel myself dropping lower during each closet session. Eventually I sank deep enough to find a new level inside me that I'd never known existed. This place is underneath; low, deep, quiet, still. There are no voices there, not even my own. All I can hear down there is my breath. It was as though I'd been drowning and in my panic I had been gasping for air, calling for rescue, and flailing on the surface. But what I really needed to do to save myself was let myself sink. It struck me that this is why we say to people, "Calm down." Because beneath the noise of the pounding, swirling surf is a place where all is quiet and clear.

Since the chaos stills in this deep, I could sense something there I was not able to sense on the surface. It was like that silent chamber in Denmark—one of the quietest places in the world—where people can actually hear and feel their own blood circulating. There, in the deep, I could sense something circulating inside me. It was a *Knowing*.

I can *know* things down at this level that I can't on the chaotic surface. Down here, when I pose a question about my life—in words or abstract images—I sense a nudge. The nudge guides me toward the next precise thing, and then, when I silently acknowledge the nudge—it fills me. The Knowing feels like warm liquid gold filling my veins and solidifying just enough to make me feel steady, certain.

What I learned (even though I am afraid to say it) is that God lives in this deepness inside me. When I recognize God's presence and guidance, God celebrates by flooding me with warm liquid gold.

Every day, I returned to the closet, sat down on the floor littered with T-shirts and jeans, and I practiced sinking. The Knowing would meet me in the deep and nudge me toward the next right thing, one thing at a time. That was how I began to know what to do next. That was how I began to walk through my life more clearly, solid and steady.

A year later, I found myself in the middle of a work meeting, sitting at a long conference table. We were discussing an important decision that had to be made, and the team was looking to me for leadership. I felt uncertain. I was about to fall back into my old way of knowing: looking outward for acceptance, permission, and consensus. But when I glanced over and caught sight of the door to the supply closet, I remembered my new way of knowing.

I wondered if the team would mind if I excused myself to spend a few minutes in that closet. Instead, I took a deep breath, and, with eyes wide open, I turned inward and tried to sink right there at the table. It worked. I sensed the nudge, and as soon as I acknowledged it, I was filled with warm liquid gold. I rose back to the surface, smiled, and said, "I know what to do."

I calmly and assuredly told the others the thing I wanted us to do. The panic in the room settled. Everyone breathed and seemed instantly relaxed and steady. We moved on.

God came out of the closet, and now I can take God anywhere.

I now take orders only from my own Knowing. Whether I'm presented with a work, personal, or family decision—a monumental or tiny decision—whenever uncertainty rises, I sink. I sink beneath the swirling surf of words, fear, expectations, conditioning, and advice—and feel for the Knowing. I sink a hundred times a day. I have to, because the Knowing never reveals a five-year plan. It feels to me like a loving, playful guide, like the reason it will only reveal the next right thing is that it wants me to come back again and again, because it wants to do life together. After many years, I'm developing a relationship with this Knowing: We are learning to trust each other.

When I talk like this, my wife raises her eyebrow and asks, "Aren't you just talking to yourself down there?" Maybe. If what I've found in the deep is just my self—if what I've learned is not how to commune with God but how to commune with myself—if who I have learned to trust is not God but myself—and if, for the rest of my life, no matter how lost I get, I know exactly where and how to find myself again—well, then. That is certainly enough of a miracle for me.

Why do we worry about *what* to call the Knowing, instead of sharing with each other *how* to call the Knowing? I know many people who have found this level inside them and live solely by it. Some call the Knowing God or wisdom or intuition or source or deepest self. I have a friend with some serious God issues, and she calls it Sebastian. A God by any other name is an equal miracle and relief. It doesn't matter *what* we call our

Knowing. What matters—if we want to live our singular shooting star of a life—is *that* we call it.

I have learned that if I want to rise, I have to sink first. I have to search for and depend upon the voice of inner wisdom instead of voices of outer approval. This saves me from living someone else's life. It also saves me a hell of a lot of time and energy. I just do the next thing the Knowing guides me toward, one thing at a time. I don't ask permission first, which is just such a grown-up way to live. The best part is this: The Knowing is beyond and beneath language, so I have no language to use to translate it to anyone. Since it doesn't use words to explain itself to me, I quit using words to explain myself to the world. This is the most revolutionary thing a woman can do: the next precise thing, one thing at a time, without asking permission or offering explanation. This way of life is thrilling.

I understand now that no one else in the world knows what I should do. The experts don't know, the ministers, the therapists, the magazines, the authors, my parents, my friends, they don't know. Not even the folks who love me the most. Because no one has ever lived or will ever live this life I am attempting to live, with my gifts and challenges and past and people. Every life is an unprecedented experiment. This life is mine alone. So I have stopped asking people for directions to places they've never been. There is no map. We are all pioneers.

I've got this second key tattooed on my wrist:

Be Still

It's my daily reminder that, if I am willing to sit in the stillness with myself, I always know what to do. That the answers are never out there. They are as close as my breath and as steady as my heartbeat. All I have to do is stop flailing, sink below the surface, and feel for the nudge and the gold. Then I have to trust it, no matter how illogical or scary the next right thing seems. Because the more consistently, bravely, and precisely I follow the inner Knowing, the more precise and beautiful my outer life becomes. The more I live by my own Knowing, the more my life becomes my own and the less afraid I become. I trust that the Knowing will go with me wherever I go, nudging me toward the next thing, one thing at a time, guiding me all the way home.

HOW TO KNOW:
Moment of uncertainty arises.
Breathe, turn inward, sink.
Feel around for the Knowing.
Do the next thing it nudges you toward.
Let it stand. (Don't explain.)
Repeat forever.

(For the rest of your life: Continue to shorten the gap between the Knowing and the doing.)

Imagine

Key Three: Dare to Imagine

When I was twenty-six years old, I found myself sitting on a dirty bathroom floor holding a positive pregnancy test. I stared at the little blue cross and thought: *Well, this is impossible. There could not be a worse candidate for motherhood on Earth.* I'd binged and purged several times a day for sixteen years. I'd been drinking myself to blackout every night for the previous seven. I'd destroyed my liver, my credit, my record, my tooth enamel, and all of my relationships. My aching head, the empty beer bottles on the floor, my bank account, my ringless, trembling fingers, they all screamed: *No. Not you.*

Yet something inside me whispered: *Yes. Me.*

All evidence to the contrary, I could *imagine* myself as a sober, thriving mother.

I became sober, and then I became a mother, a wife, and a writer.

Fast-forward fourteen years. Reminder: I'm forty years old

now. I've got one husband, two dogs, and three children who adore their father. I also have a skyrocketing writing career, based partly on my traditional family and Christianity. I'm at an event to launch my new book, the highly anticipated memoir about my marriage's redemption. At that event, a woman walks into the room, and I look at her and fall madly in love within the same moment. My circumstances, my fear, my religion, my career—they all scream: *No. Not her.*

And yet something inside me whispered: *Yes. Her.*

The something inside me was my imagination.

All evidence to the contrary, I could *imagine* myself as Abby's partner. I could imagine the kind of love in which I was fully seen, known, and cherished.

The facts were right there in front of me to see.

But the truth was right there inside of me to feel.

Swelling, pressing, insisting: *There is a life meant for you that is truer than the one you're living. But in order to have it, you will have to forge it yourself. You will have to create on the outside what you are imagining on the inside. Only you can bring it forth. And it will cost you everything.*

I have learned to live by faith, which does not mean that I live by a set of unwavering beliefs or dogma that men laid down ages ago to keep their power by controlling others. My faith has nothing to do with religion anymore. To me, living by faith is allowing the swelling and pressing inside me to direct my outward words and decisions. Because to me, God is not a being outside of me: God is the fire, the nudge, the warm liquid gold swelling and pressing inside me.

In fact, my favorite idea of faith is *a belief in the unseen order of things.*

There are two orders of things:

There is the *seen order* unfolding in front of us every day on our streets and in the news. In this visible order, violence reigns and children are shot in their schools and warmongers prosper and 1 percent of the world hoards half of all we have. We call this order of things reality. This is "the way things are." It's all we can see because it's all we've ever seen. Yet something inside us rejects it. We know instinctively: This is not the intended order of things. This is not how things are meant to be. We know that there is a better, truer, wilder way.

That better way is the *unseen order* inside us. It is the vision we carry in our imagination about a truer, more beautiful world—one in which all children have enough to eat and we no longer kill each other and mothers do not have to cross deserts with their babies on their backs. This better idea is what Jews call shalom, Buddhists call nirvana, Christians call heaven, Muslims call salaam, and many agnostics call peace. It is not a place *out there*—not yet; it's the hopeful swelling *in here,* pressing through our skin, insisting that it was all meant to be more beautiful than this. And it can be, if we refuse to wait to die and "go to heaven" and instead find heaven inside us and give birth to it here and now. If we work to make the vision of the unseen order swelling inside us visible in our lives, homes, and nations, we will make reality more beautiful. On Earth as it is in heaven. In our material world as it is in our imagination.

Tabitha.

She was born into captivity. The only visible order she's ever known includes cages and dirty pink bunnies and weak, bored applause. Tabitha never knew the wild. Yet Tabitha *knew the wild*. It was *in* her. She sensed the pressing of the unseen order like a relentless hunch. Perhaps for us, as for Tabitha, the deepest truth is not what we can see but what we can imagine.

Perhaps imagination is not where we go to escape reality but where we go to remember it. Perhaps when we want to know the original plan for our lives, families, world, we should consult not what's in front of us but what's inside us.

Imagination is how personal and worldwide revolutions begin.

"I have a dream," said Martin Luther King, Jr.

"Dreaming, after all, is a form of planning," said Gloria Steinem.

In order to move our culture forward, revolutionaries have had to speak and plan from the unseen order inside them. For those of us who were not consulted in the building of the visible order, igniting our imagination is the only way to see beyond what was created to leave us out. If those who were not part of the building of reality only consult reality for possibilities, reality will never change. We will keep shuffling and competing for a seat at their table instead of building our own tables. We will keep banging our heads on their glass ceilings instead of pitching our own huge tent outside. We will remain caged by this world instead of taking our rightful place as co-creators of it.

Each of us was born to bring forth something that has never existed: a way of being, a family, an idea, art, a community—something brand-new. We are here to fully introduce ourselves, to impose ourselves and ideas and thoughts and dreams onto the world, leaving it changed forever by who we are and what we bring forth from our depths. So we cannot contort ourselves to fit into the visible order. We must unleash ourselves and watch the world reorder itself in front of our eyes.

My job is to listen deeply to women. What many tell me is that they harbor an achy, heavy hunch that their lives, relationships, and world were meant to be more beautiful than they are.

They ask, "Shouldn't my marriage feel more loving than this? Shouldn't my religion be more alive and kind than this? Shouldn't my work be more meaningful and my community be more connected? Shouldn't the world I'm leaving to my babies be less brutal? Isn't it all just supposed to be more beautiful than this?"

The women asking these questions remind me of Tabitha. They are stalking the periphery of their lives, feeling discontent. To me, this is exciting, because discontent is the nagging of the imagination. Discontent is evidence that your imagination has not given up on you. It is still pressing, swelling, trying to get your attention by whispering: "Not this."

"Not this" is a very important stage.

But knowing what we do not want is not the same as knowing what we do want.

So how can we get from *Not this* to *This instead*? How can we move from *feeling* discontent to *creating* new lives and new worlds? In other words: How can we begin to live from our imagination instead of our indoctrination?

Language is my favorite tool, so I use it to help people build a bridge between what's in front of them and what's inside them. I have learned that if we want to hear the voice of imagination, we must speak to it in the language it understands.

If we want to know who we were meant to be before the world told us who to be—

If we want to know where we were meant to go before we were put in our place—

If we want to taste freedom instead of control—

Then we must relearn our soul's native tongue.

When women write to me in the language of indoctrination—when they use words like *good* and *should* and *right* and *wrong*—I try to speak back to them in the language of imagination.

We are all bilingual. We speak the language of indoctrination, but our native tongue is the language of imagination. When we use the language of indoctrination—with its *should* and *shouldn't*, *right* and *wrong*, *good* and *bad*—we are activating our minds. That's not what we're going for here. Because our minds are polluted by our training. In order to get beyond our training, we need to activate our imaginations. Our minds are excuse makers; our imaginations are storytellers. So instead of asking ourselves what's right or wrong, we must ask ourselves:

What is true and beautiful?

Then our imagination rises inside us, thanks us for finally consulting it after all these years, and tells us a story.

Clare wrote to me recently. She's a lawyer and the daughter of an alcoholic. When she sat down to email me, she had just woken up, still woozy from her nightly "take the edge off" glasses of wine. She wrote that she spends most of her time numb or foggy or ashamed. "G, I feel like I'm wasting my life," she wrote. "What should I do?"

"Clare," I wrote. "What is the truest, most beautiful story about your life you can imagine?"

Sasha wrote to tell me about her marriage. She married a guy who is distant and cold, just like her father had been. Sasha spent most of her days hustling to earn her husband's love, just like her mom had done to earn her dad's. She wrote, "I'm so tired and lonely. What's the right thing to do here?"

I replied, "Sasha, can you tell me a story about the truest, most beautiful marriage you can imagine?"

Danielle, a thirty-four-year-old former kindergarten teacher, wrote to me recently. She spends her days and nights watching her seven-year-old die slowly in her arms, tortured by the same disease that killed her first son three years ago. Night and day, she sits by her son's bedside—feeding him, singing to him, soothing him. "I'm broken, Glennon," she wrote. "I don't know what to do."

I wrote back, "Danielle, what is the truest, most beautiful story you can imagine about a mother and her sons?"

Each of them replied to me. Clare wrote a story about a woman who never abandoned herself, who faced life on life's terms and was present for herself, her people, her life. She believed in that vision enough to begin therapy and to safely let rise to the surface all the pain she was trying to drown out with wine. Months later she wrote to say that her new way of being is harder than ever, but it's the right kind of hard. She's not missing her own life anymore. When she looks at herself in the mirror, she no longer needs to look away. She is now a woman who can look into her own eyes.

Sasha spent several evenings writing a story about the truest, most beautiful marriage she could imagine. She spent a week mustering the courage to send it to me because she was scared to let someone on the outside see what was on her inside. Eventually she printed it out and left it on her husband's pillow. She was heartbroken when he didn't mention it for three weeks. Then, one night, she found an invitation from him, asking her to go to a marriage retreat. They could both imagine something more beautiful, it turned out. They were ready to try to make it real.

Danielle wrote back to me from her son's hospital bedside after I asked her about the truest, most beautiful story about parenting she could imagine.

She said this: "I've spent the past week considering your question. I can imagine a thousand easier stories about mothers and sons. I can think of a million happier ones. But I cannot imagine a single story truer or more beautiful than the heartbreaking one I'm living now, with my boys."

"Me neither," I wrote back. "Me neither."

The truest, most beautiful life never promises to be an easy one. We need to let go of the lie that it's supposed to be.

Each of those women has begun to live from her imagination. Here's how: Each honored her own discontent. She did not dismiss it, bury it, deflect it, deny it, blame it on someone else, or tell herself to shut up and be grateful. She heard her Knowing whisper "Not this," and she admitted to herself that she heard it. She sat with it for a while. Then she dared to utter her inner whisper out loud. She shared her discontent with another human being.

Then, when she was ready to move from *Not this* to *This instead,* she dared to call upon her imagination to tell her the story she was born to tell with her life. She dreamed up what it would look like to have her specific version of truth and beauty come to life. She looked for the blueprint she'd been born with, the one she'd forgotten existed. She unearthed her unseen order: her original plan.

Then—and this is crucial—she put pen to paper. The people who build their truest, most beautiful lives usually do. It's hard to jump from dreaming to doing. As every architect or designer knows, there is a critical step between vision and reality. Before imagination becomes three-dimensional, it usually needs to become two-dimensional. It's as though the unseen order needs to come to life one dimension at a time.

Women have sent me so many of their two-dimensional dreams over the years. They say: "For me, the truest, most beautiful life, family, world looks like . . ."

I marvel at how wildly different each of their stories is. It's proof that our lives were never meant to be cookie-cutter, culturally constructed carbon copies of some ideal. There is no one way to live, love, raise children, arrange a family, run a school, a community, a nation. The norms were created by somebody, and each of us is somebody. We can make our own normal. We can throw out all the rules and write our own. We can build our lives from the inside out. We can stop asking what the world wants from us and instead ask ourselves what we want for our world. We can stop looking at what's in front of us long enough to discover what's inside us. We can remember and unleash the life-changing, relationship-changing, world-changing power of our own imagination. It might take us a lifetime. Luckily, a lifetime is exactly how long we have.

Let's conjure up, from the depths of our souls:

The truest, most beautiful lives we can imagine.

The truest, most beautiful families we can fathom.

The truest, most beautiful world we can hope for.

Let's put it all on paper.

Let's look at what we've written and decide that these are not pipe dreams; these are our marching orders. These are the blueprints for our lives, our families, and the world.

May the invisible order become visible.

May our dreams become our plans.

Let It Burn

Key Four: Build and Burn

When we let ourselves feel, our inner self transforms. When we act upon our Knowing and imagination, our outer worlds transform. Living from the worlds within us will change our outer worlds. Here's the rub: Destruction is essential to construction. If we want to build the new, we must be willing to let the old burn. We must be committed to holding on to nothing but the truth. We must decide that if the truth inside us can burn a belief, a family structure, a business, a religion, an industry—it should have become ashes yesterday.

If we feel, know, and imagine—our lives, families, and world become truer versions of themselves. *Eventually.* But at first it's very scary. Because once we feel, know, and dare to imagine more for ourselves, we cannot unfeel, unknow, or un-imagine. There is no going back. We are launched into the abyss—the space between the not-true-enough life we're living and the truer one that exists only inside us. So we say, "Maybe it's safer to just stay here. Even if it's not true enough, maybe it's good enough." But good enough is what makes people drink too much and snark too much and become bitter and sick and live in quiet desperation until they lie on their deathbed and wonder: *What kind of life/relationship/family/world might I have created if I'd been braver?*

The building of the true and beautiful means the destruction of the good enough. Rebirth means death. Once a truer, more beautiful vision is born inside us, *life* is in the direction of that vision. Holding on to what is no longer true enough is not safe; it's the riskiest move because it is the certain death of everything that was meant to be. We are alive only to the degree to which we are willing to be annihilated. Our next life will always cost us this one. If we are truly alive, we are constantly losing who we just were, what we just built, what we just believed, what we just knew to be true.

I have lost identities, beliefs, and relationships it has hurt to lose. I have learned that when I live from my emotions, knowing, and imagination, I am always losing. What I lose is always what is no longer true enough so that I can take full hold of what is.

For a long while I contorted myself to live according to a set of old memos I'd been issued about how to become a successful woman and build a strong family, career, and faith. I thought those memos were universal Truth, so I abandoned myself to honor them *without even unearthing and examining them*. When I finally pulled them out of my subconscious and looked hard at them: I learned that these memos had never been Truth at all—just my particular culture's arbitrary expectations. Hustling to comply with my memos, I was flying on autopilot, routed to a destination I never chose. So I took back the wheel. I quit abandoning myself to honor those memos. Instead, I

abandoned the memos and began honoring myself. I began to
live as a woman who never got the world's memos.

I burned the memo that defined selflessness as the pinnacle
of womanhood, but first I forgave myself for believing that lie
for so long. I had abandoned myself out of love. They'd convinced me that the best way for a woman to love her partner,
family, and community was to lose herself in service to them.
In my desire to be of service, I did myself and the world a great
disservice. I've seen what happens out in the world and inside
our relationships when women stay numb, obedient, quiet,
and small. Selfless women make for an efficient society but not
a beautiful, true, or just one. When women lose themselves,
the world loses its way. We do not need more selfless women.
What we need right now is more women who have detoxed
themselves so completely from the world's expectations that
they are full of nothing but themselves. What we need are
women who are *full of themselves*. A woman who is full of herself knows and trusts herself enough to say and do what must
be done. She lets the rest burn.

I burned the memo presenting responsible motherhood as
martyrdom. I decided that the call of motherhood is to become
a model, not a martyr. I unbecame a mother slowly dying in
her children's name and became a responsible mother: one who
shows her children how to be fully alive.

I burned the memo insisting that the way a family avoids
brokenness is to keep its structure by any means necessary. I
noticed families clinging to their original structures that were
very broken, indeed. I noticed other families whose structures
had shifted and were healthy and vibrant. I decided that a family's wholeness or brokenness has little to do with its structure.
A broken family is a family in which any member must break
herself into pieces to fit in. A whole family is one in which each

member can bring her full self to the table knowing that she will always be both held and free.

I decided to let my family's form become an evolving eco-system. I unbecame a woman clinging to a prescribed family structure and became one clinging to each of her family member's right to their full humanity: including me. We would break and rebreak our structure instead of allowing any of us to live broken.

I quit buying the idea that a successful marriage is one that lasts till death, even if one or both spouses are dying inside it. I decided that before I ever vowed myself to another person, I'd take this vow to myself: I'll not abandon myself. Not ever again. Me and myself: We are till death do us part. We'll forsake all others to remain whole. I unbecame a woman who believed that another would complete me when I decided that I was born complete.

I let burn my cherished, comfortable idea of America as a place of liberty and justice for all. I let a truer, wider perspective be born in its place, one that included the American experience of people who don't look like me.

I wrote myself a new memo about what it means to have strong faith. To me, faith is not a public allegiance to a set of outer beliefs, but a private surrender to the inner Knowing. I stopped believing in middlemen or hierarchy between me and God. I went from certain and defensive to curious, wide-eyed, and awed; from closed fists to open arms; from the shallow to the deep end. For me, living in faith means allowing to burn all that separates me from the Knowing so that one day I can say: *I and the Mother are one.*

The memos I've written for myself are neither right nor wrong; they are just mine. They're written in sand so that I can revise them whenever I feel, know, imagine a truer, more beautiful idea for myself. I'll be revising them until I take my last breath.

I am a human being, meant to be in perpetual becoming. If I am living bravely, my entire life will become a million deaths and rebirths. My goal is not to remain the same but to live in such a way that each day, year, moment, relationship, conversation, and crisis is the material I use to become a truer, more beautiful version of myself. The goal is to surrender, constantly, who I just was in order to become who this next moment calls me to be. I will not hold on to a single existing idea, opinion, identity, story, or relationship that keeps me from emerging new. I cannot hold too tightly to any riverbank. I must let go of the shore in order to travel deeper and see farther. Again and again and then again. Until the final death and rebirth. Right up until then.

part three
free

aches

I'm thirteen years old and bulimic, so I spend half my life curling my bangs and the other half eating excessively and throwing up. Curling and hurling are not an acceptable life, so on Fridays after school my mom drives me downtown to the therapist. She stays in the lobby and I walk in alone, sit down in a brown leather chair, and wait for the therapist to ask, "How are you today, Glennon?"

I smile and say, "I'm fine. How are *you* today?" She breathes deeply with her whole body. Then we're quiet.

I notice a picture of a small redheaded girl on my kind, frustrated therapist's desk. I ask who the girl is. She glances over, touches the frame, and says, "That's my daughter." When she turns back to me, her face is sad and soft. She says, "Glennon, you say you're fine, but you aren't. Your eating disorder could kill you. You know that. What you don't know is that since you refuse to feel all of this, since you won't join us in the land of the living, you're half dead already."

I am offended. My insides turn hot and they feel instantly

inflated, difficult to contain. I hold my breath and clench everything.

"Well, maybe I'm *trying* to be fine. Maybe *all I do* is try to be fine. Maybe I try harder than anybody."

She says, "Maybe you should stop trying to be fine. Maybe life isn't fine, and maybe it'll never be fine. Maybe fine isn't the right goal. What if you stopped trying so hard to be fine and just . . . lived?"

"I don't know what you're talking about," I say.

I know exactly what she's talking about. She's talking about the Ache.

I don't know when I first discovered the Ache, but by the time I am ten years old, it has become my constant interrupter.

When my cat, Co-Co, climbs onto the couch with me, she rubs her face against mine so softly and she purrs so gently that I'm tempted to let myself melt into her. But the Ache interrupts with: *Be careful. She won't live very long. You'll have to bury her soon.*

When my grandmother Alice whispers her evening rosary, I spy on her. She is the master of the universe, there in her rocker, controlling everything on Earth, keeping me safe. Just as I become lulled into peace by the rocking, the Ache points and says: *Look at how bruised and papery the skin on her hands is. See how they shake?*

When my mom leans over to kiss me good night, I catch the smell of her face lotion. I feel the soft sheets under me and the warm blanket around me, and I breathe in deeply. I rarely make it to the exhale in peace, though. The Ache paralyzes me with *You know how this ends. When she goes, you will not survive.*

I don't know if the Ache is trying to protect me or terrorize me. I don't know if it loves me or hates me, if it's bad or good. I just know that its role is to constantly remind me of the most essential fact of life, which is: *This ends. Don't get too attached to anything.* So when I get too soft, too comforted, too close to love, the Ache reminds me. It always arrives in words (she'll die) or an image (a phone call, a funeral), and immediately, my body responds. I stiffen, hold my breath, straighten my spine, break eye contact, lean away. After that, I'm in control again. The Ache keeps me prepared, distant, safe. The Ache keeps me fine, which is another word for half dead.

It takes a lot of effort for a live human being to stay half dead. For me, it also takes a lot of food. When I discover bingeing and purging at ten, food addiction becomes a whole life I can lead that has utterly nothing to do with actual life. Bulimia keeps me busy, distant, distracted. I plan my next binge all day, and when I find a private place to start eating, my frenzy becomes a raging waterfall inside and outside me—loud, much too loud, for any interruption at all. There is no remembering, no Ache, nothing but the binge. Then, just as I'm stuffed to the point of more nothingness, the purge. Another waterfall. More noise. Nothing but noise until I am on the floor, laid out, wracked, too tired to feel or think or remember anything at all. Perfect.

Bulimia is private. I need a way to silence the Ache in public, too. That's what booze is for. Booze overpowers the Ache. Instead of just interrupting love, it blocks it completely. No connection is real, so there is nothing risky for the Ache to bother interrupting. Over the years I learn that the bonus of booze is that it destroys all of my relationships before I can. You can't lose people who never even found you.

By the time I turn twenty-five, I have been arrested repeatedly. I cough up blood on a regular basis. My family has distanced themselves from me for their own protection. I have no feelings left, and I am nowhere near the land of the living, which is for fools and masochists. I am no fool. I have beaten life at its own game. I have learned how to exist without living at all, and I am completely free—with nothing left to lose. I am also almost dead, but by God, I am safe. Take that, Life.

And then, that May morning, I find myself staring at that positive pregnancy test. I am certainly surprised by the pregnancy, but I'm absolutely stunned by my reaction to it. I feel inside me a deep desire to grow and birth and raise a person.

These thoughts are foreign and baffling. I stand up and stare at my puffy, dirty face in the mirror and think: *Hold up. Wait, what? You, there in the mirror. You don't even LIKE life. You don't even find it worth trying yourself. Why, then, are you suddenly desperate to bestow life upon another being as though it's some kind of gift?*

The only answer I have is: Because I love it already. I want life for this being because I love this being. Why don't I want life for myself, then? I want to be a being that I love, too.

The Ache sweeps in with a ferocity. *Danger! Danger! Don't be ridiculous!* It becomes difficult to breathe. Yet there in that bathroom—dirty, sick, broken, aching, gasping—I still want to become a mother. That is how I learn that there is something deeper and truer and more powerful inside me than the Ache. Because the deeper thing wins. The deeper thing is my desire to become a mother. This is what I want more than I want to stay safe: I want to be this being's mother.

I decide, right there on the floor, to get sober and reenter the land of the living. I suspect that the courage I muster up to make this decision is due, in large part, to the fact that I'm still wasted from the night before. I stand up and wobble out of the bathroom and into life.

Life is exactly as I remembered it: just the fucking worst.

While I attempt to both *become* a human and *grow* a human at the exact same ridiculous time, I am also teaching third grade. By noon each day, I am dizzy with several sicknesses at once: morning sickness, withdrawal sickness, and the sickness of living without a daily escape plan. Each day at noon, I walk my class the long way to lunch so I can peek into my friend Josie's classroom and see the sign hung above her window, which says in big black block letters: WE CAN DO HARD THINGS.

"We can do hard things" becomes my hourly life mantra. It is my affirmation that living life on life's own absurd terms *is* hard. It isn't hard because I'm weak or flawed or because I made a wrong turn somewhere, it is hard because life is just hard for humans and I am a human who is finally doing life right. "We can do hard things" insists that I can, and should, stay in the hard because there is some kind of reward for staying. I don't know what the reward is yet, but it feels true that there would be one, and I want to find out what it is. I am especially comforted by the *We* part. I don't know who the *We* is; I just need to believe that there is a *We* somewhere, either helping me through my hard things or doing their own hard things while I do mine.

This is how I survive early sobriety, which turns out to be one long Return of the Ache. I say to myself every few minutes: *This is hard. We can do hard things.* And then I do them.

Fast-forward ten years. I have three children, a husband, a house, and a big career as a writer. I am not just a sober, upstanding citizen, I am kind of *fancy,* honestly. I am, by all accounts, humaning successfully. At a book signing during that time, a reporter approaches my father, points toward the long line of people waiting to meet me, and says, "You must be so proud of your daughter." My father looks at the reporter and says, "Honestly, we're just happy she's not in jail." We are all so happy I'm not in jail.

One morning, I am in my closet, getting dressed, when my phone rings. I answer. It's my sister. She is speaking slowly and deliberately because she is between contractions. She says, "It's time, Sissy. The baby's coming. Can you fly to Virginia now?"

I say, "Yes, I can. I will come! I will be there soon!" Then I hang up and stare at a large stack of jeans on my shelf. I am unsure of what to do next. During the past decade I have learned how to do many hard things, but I still don't know how to do easy things, like book a flight. My sister usually does easy things for me. I think and think and decide that it is perhaps a less-than-ideal time to call her back and ask if she's aware of any good airline deals. I think some more and begin to wonder if anyone else's sister might be available to help me. Then the phone rings again. This time it's my mom. Her voice is slow and deliberate, too. She says, "Honey. You need to come to Ohio right away. It's time to say good-bye to Grandma."

I say nothing.

She says, "Honey? Are you there? Are you okay?"

How are you today, Glennon?

I'm am still in my closet, staring at my jeans. That's what I remember thinking first: *I have a lot of jeans.*

Then the Ache becomes real and knocks on my door. My grandma Alice is dying. I am being called to fly *toward* the dying.

How are you today, Glennon?

I do not say, "I'm fine, Mom."

I say, "I'm not okay, but I am coming. I love you."

I hang up, walk to my computer, and google "how to buy plane tickets." I accidentally buy three tickets, but I am still proud of myself. I walk back into my closet and begin to pack. I am both packing and watching myself pack, and my watching self is saying: *Wow. Look at you. You are doing it. You look like a grown-up. Don't stop, don't think, just keep moving. We can do hard things.*

Surprisingly, now that the Ache has transformed from idea

to reality, I feel relatively steady. Dealing with the dropped shoe is less paralyzing, apparently, than waiting for that shoe to drop.

I call my sister and tell her I have to go to Ohio first. She already knows. My mom picks me up at the Cleveland airport and drives me to the retirement home. We are quiet and soft with each other. No one says she's fine. We arrive and walk through the loud lobby, then through the antiseptic-smelling hallway and into my grandmother's warm, dark, Catholic room. I pass her motorized wheelchair and notice the gray duct tape covering the "high-speed" button, which she lost her right to use when her hallway velocity began scaring the other residents. I sit down in the chair next to my grandmother's bed. I touch the Mary statue on her bedside table, then the deep blue glass rosary beads draped over Mary's hands. I peek behind the table and see a small calendar hung there, the theme of which is hot priests. Each month's priest wears a full vestment and a smoldering smile. This calendar is a fund-raiser for something or other. Charity has always been important to my grandmother. My mother stands several feet behind me, giving my grandmother and me time and space.

I have never in my life felt the Ache more deeply than I do in that moment, as my mother stands behind me, watching me touch each of her mother's things, knowing exactly which memory I am recalling with each lingering touch. Knowing that her daughter is preparing to say good-bye to her mother and that her mother is preparing to say good-bye to her daughter.

My grandmother reaches over, rests her hand on mine, and looks at me deeply.

This is when the Ache becomes too powerful to resist. I am out of practice. I don't stiffen. I don't hold my breath. I don't break eye contact. I unclench and let it take me.

First it takes me to the thought that one day, not long from now, these roles will shift. I will be in my mother's place, watching my daughter say good-bye to my mother. Then, not too long from then, it will be my daughter, watching her daughter say good-bye to me. I think these thoughts. I see these visions. I feel them, too. They are hard and deep.

The Ache continues to take me with it, and now I am somewhere else. I am in the Ache. I am in the One Big Ache of lovepainbeautytendernesslonginggoodbye and I am here with my grandmother and my mother, and suddenly I understand that I am here with everyone else, too. Somehow I am here with everyone who has ever lived and ever loved and ever lost. I have entered the place I thought was death, and it has turned out to be life itself. I entered this Ache alone, but inside it I have found everyone. In surrendering to the Ache of loneliness I have discovered un-loneliness. Right here, inside the Ache, with everyone who has ever welcomed a child or held the hand of a dying grandmother or said good-bye to a great love. I am here, with all of them. Here is the "We" that I recognized in Josie's sign. Inside the Ache is the "We." We can do hard things, like be alive and love deep and lose it all, because we do these hard things alongside everyone who has ever walked the Earth with her eyes, arms, and heart wide open.

The Ache is not a flaw. The Ache is our meeting place. It's the clubhouse of the brave. All the lovers are there. It is where you go alone to meet the world. The Ache is love.

The Ache was never warning me: *This ends, so leave.* She was saying: *This ends, so stay.*

I stayed. I held my grandmother Alice Flaherty's paper hands. I touched the wedding rings she still wore twenty-six years after my grandfather's death. "I love you, honey," she said. "I love you too, Grandma," I said. "Take care of that baby for me," she said.

That was it. I did not say anything remarkable at all. It turns out that a lot of good-bye is done in the touching of things: rosaries, hands, memories, love. I kissed my grandmother, felt her warm, soft forehead with my lips. Then I stood up and walked out of the room. My mother followed me. She shut the door behind us, and we stood in the hallway and held each other and shook. We had taken a great journey together, to the place where brave people go, and it had changed us.

My mom drove me back to the airport. I boarded another plane to Virginia. My dad picked me up, and we drove to the birthing center. I walked into my sister's room, and she looked over at me from her bed. Then she looked down at the bundle in her arms and up at me again. She said, "Sister, meet your niece, Alice Flaherty."

I took baby Alice into my arms, and we sat down in the rocking chair next to my sister's bed. First I touched Alice Flaherty's hands. Purple and papery. Next I noticed her gray-blue eyes, which stared right into mine. They looked like the eyes of the master of the universe. They said to me: *Hello. Here I am. Life goes on.*

Since I got sober, I have never been fine again, not for a single moment. I have been exhausted and terrified and angry. I have been overwhelmed and underwhelmed and debilitatingly depressed and anxious. I have been amazed and awed and delighted and overjoyed to bursting. I have been reminded, constantly, by the Ache: *This will pass; stay close.*

I have been alive.

ghosts

I was born a little broken, with an extra dose of sensitivity.
—SOME HORSESHIT I WROTE ABOUT MYSELF
IN MY FIRST MEMOIR

When I was in my twenties, I believed that somewhere there existed a perfect human woman. She woke up beautiful, unbloated, clear skinned, fluffy haired, fearless, lucky in love, calm, and confident. Her life was . . . easy. She haunted me like a ghost. I tried so hard to be her.

In my thirties, I gave that ghost the finger. I quit trying to be the perfect woman and decided to "celebrate my imperfection." I claimed a new identity: Jacked-Up Human! I announced to anyone who would listen, "I'm a hot mess and proud of it! I love this crappy version of humanity that I am! I am broken and beautiful!! Eff you, Perfect Woman!"

The problem was that I still believed that there was an ideal human and that I was not her. The problem was that I still believed in ghosts. I had just decided to live in defiance of perfection instead of in pursuit of it. Rebellion is as much of a cage as obedience is. They both mean living in reaction to someone else's way instead of forging your own. Freedom is not being for or against an ideal, but creating your own existence from scratch.

A few years ago, Oprah Winfrey was interviewing me about my first memoir. She opened the book and read my words back to me: *I was born a little broken.* Then she paused, looked up from the page, and asked, "Would you still describe yourself that way? As broken?" Her eyes sparkled. I looked at her and said, "No, actually. I wouldn't. That's ridiculous. I think this sort of thing is why Jesus only wrote in the sand."

Broken means: *does not function as it was designed to function.* A broken human is one who *does not function the way humans are designed to function.* When I think about my own human experience, what honest people have told me about their human experiences, and the experiences of every historical and contemporary human being I've ever studied, we all seem to function in the exact same way:

We hurt people, and we are hurt by people. We feel left out, envious, not good enough, sick, and tired. We have unrealized dreams and deep regrets. We are certain that we were meant for more and that we don't even deserve what we have. We feel ecstatic and then numb. We wish our parents had done better by us. We wish we could do better by our children. We betray and we are betrayed. We lie and we are lied to. We say good-bye to animals, to places, to people we cannot live without. We are so afraid of dying. Also: of living. We have fallen in love and out of love, and people have fallen in love and out of love with us. We wonder if what happened to us that night will mean we can never be touched again without fear. We live with rage bubbling. We are sweaty, bloated, gassy, oily. We love our children, we long for children, we do not want children. We are at war with our bodies, our minds, our souls. We are at war with one another. We wish we'd said all those things while they were still here. They're still here, and we're still not saying those things. We know we won't. We don't understand ourselves. We don't understand why we hurt those we love. We want to be forgiven. We cannot forgive. We don't understand God. We believe. We absolutely do not believe. We are lonely. We want to be left alone. We want to belong. We want to be loved. We want to be loved. We want to be loved.

If this is our shared human experience, where did we get the idea that there is some other, better, more perfect, unbroken way to be human? Where is the human being who is functioning "correctly," against whom we are all judging our performances? Who is she? *Where* is she? What is her life if it is not these things?

I got free the moment I realized that my problem isn't that I'm not a good enough human; my problem is that I'm not a good enough ghost. Since I don't have to be a ghost, I don't have a problem.

If you are uncomfortable—in deep pain, angry, yearning, confused—you don't have a problem, you have a life. Being human is not hard because you're doing it wrong, it's hard because you're doing it right. You will never change the fact that being human is hard, so you must change your idea that it was ever supposed to be easy.

I will not call myself broken, flawed, or imperfect anymore. I will quit chasing ghosts, because the chase left me weary. And because I am a woman who no longer believes in ghosts.

Allow me to rewrite my own self-description:

I am forty-four years old. With all my chin hairs and pain and contradictions, I am flawless, unbroken. There is no other way.

I am haunted by nothing.

smiles

Two Christmases ago, my sister and I presented our parents with a check to buy themselves a trip to Paris. They were so touched and proud that they framed the check, uncashed, and hung it on their living room wall. This year we doubled down. We bought four plane tickets to Paris and decided to hand deliver our parents to the city they had always wanted to visit. We stayed in a tiny apartment overlooking the Eiffel Tower. I had never been to Europe before. I was charmed.

Paris is elegant and old. Being there made me feel elegant and young. It helped me forgive America for our arrogance and fury. In Paris, surrounded by ruins of ancient baths, guillotines, and churches more than a thousand years old, humanity's mistakes and beauty are unfurled like a mural. In America, we are so new. We still fancy ourselves conquerors and renegades. We're all still trying to be the "firsts" to do this or that. Can you imagine? We are all competing for our parents' attention, and we have no parents. It makes us a little jumpy. Paris is not jumpy. Paris is calm and certain. It's not going to startle easily, and it already knows the words to all the songs. Everywhere I looked in Paris, I found proof that leaders come and go, buildings are built and fall, revolutions begin and end; nothing—no matter how grand—lasts. Paris says: We are here for such a short time. We might as well sit down for a long while with some good coffee, company, and bread. Here, there is more time to be human, maybe because there has been more time to learn how.

When we visited the Louvre, we entered the *Mona Lisa* room and found a crowd of hundreds pushing, jostling, selfieing all around her.

I stared from a distance, trying to appreciate her. I really didn't understand what all the fuss was about. I wondered if all the jostling people understood or if they were just acting like they did. A woman walked over and stood next to me.

She said, "You know, there's a theory about her smile. Want to hear it?"

"Yes, please," I said.

"Mona Lisa and her husband lost a baby. Sometime later, her husband commissioned this painting from da Vinci to celebrate the birth of another baby. Mona Lisa sat for Leonardo to paint her, but she wouldn't smile during the sitting. Not all the way. The story goes that da Vinci wanted her to smile wider, but she refused. She did not want the joy she felt for her new baby to erase the pain she felt from losing the first. There in her half smile is her half joy. Or maybe it's her full joy and her full grief all at the same time. She has the look of a woman who has just realized a dream but still carries the lost dream inside her. She wanted her whole life to be present on her face. She wanted everyone to remember, so she wouldn't pretend."

Now I understand what the fuss is all about. Mona Lisa is the patron saint of honest, resolute, fully human women— women who feel and who know. She is saying for us:

Don't tell me to smile.

I will not be pleasant.

Even trapped here, inside two dimensions, you will see the truth.

You will see my life's brutal and beautiful right here on my face.

The world will not be able to stop staring.

goals

When I got pregnant with Chase and quit drinking, drugging, and purging, I thought it might be my last chance to stop being bad and start being good. I married Chase's father, and I learned to cook and clean and fake orgasms. I was a good wife. I had three babies and put all their needs so far ahead of my own that I forgot I had needs at all. I was a good mom. I started going to church and learned to fear God and not ask too many questions of folks who claimed to represent God. I was a good Christian. I watched beauty trends carefully, and I dyed my hair and paid to get poison injected into my forehead so I wouldn't look too tired from all the effort it takes to be good at beauty. I started writing and released bestsellers and spoke to sold-out audiences all over the country. A woman isn't allowed to do well unless she also does good, so I became a do-gooder for the world. I raised tens of millions of dollars for people who were hurting, and I lost a decade of sleep writing back to strangers.

You are a *good* woman, Glennon, they said.

I was. I was so good. I was also exhausted, anxious, and lost. I assumed that was because I wasn't good enough yet; I just had to try a little harder.

My husband's infidelity was a jagged gift, because it forced me to see that being a good wife wasn't enough to keep my marriage together. Being a good mother wasn't enough to keep my kids from pain. Being a good world saver wasn't enough to save my own world.

Being bad had almost killed me. But so had being good.

I was talking to a dear friend around that time. She said, "G, remember that amazing Steinbeck quote? 'And now that you don't have to be perfect, you can be good.' I've kept it on my desk for years. I looked at it last night and thought: I'm tired of being good. I'm so tired.

"Let's change it to:

"And now that we don't have to be good, we can be free."

adam and keys

A few years ago, Alicia Keys announced to the world that she was done wearing makeup. She said, "I don't want to cover up anymore. Not my face, not my mind, not my soul, not my thoughts, not my dreams, not my struggles . . . Nothing."

That's it, I thought.

A while later, I read an interview with Adam Levine. He said that while they were filming a show together, he poked his head into Alicia Keys's dressing room. She had her back to him, and she was leaning into the mirror, putting on lipstick.

He smiled and said, "Oh! I thought Alicia doesn't wear makeup."

She turned around, looked at him, lipstick in her hand.

She said, "I do what the fuck I want."

That's it.

ears

My daughters are different. I raised Tish while I was still trying to be a good parent, but then I got tired. By the time Amma exited the birth canal, I just handed her an iPad and wished the child godspeed on her journey. One way to describe Amma is *independent*. Another is *on her own*. This parenting approach (retreat?) has served her well. She wears what she wants and says what she wants, and mostly she does what she wants. She has created herself, and she is a glorious invention with which she is well pleased.

Recently we were sitting around the kitchen table, and Tish mentioned her need to train more if she ever hoped to be great at soccer. We asked Amma if she felt the same way. Amma took a bite of her pizza and said, "Nah. I'm already great." She is *twelve*. Maybe eleven, actually. I have three children, and their ages change every single year. All I know is they are in the phase that comes after crawling but before college. Somewhere in that sweet spot.

Years ago, when I was in the thick of deciding whether I

wanted to save or end my marriage, the girls began begging to get their ears pierced. I was grateful for the distraction, so I said yes. I took them to the mall, and when we arrived at the piercing kiosk, Amma ran ahead of me, leaped into the piercing chair, and announced to the surprised twentysomething piercer, "Let's do this." When I finally caught up, the piercer turned to me and said, "Are you her mother?"

"I am trying to be," I said.

"Okay, do you want me to pierce her ears one at a time or both at the same time?"

Amma said, "Both. Do it! Let's GO!" Then she squinted her eyes, gritted her teeth, and flexed all her muscles, like a tiny Hulk. As they pierced her, I saw a couple of tears that she wiped away immediately. I looked at Amma and thought: *She is so awesome. She is also six years from a felony.* She jumped down from the chair, buzzing with adrenaline.

The women working at the kiosk laughed and said, "Wow! She is so brave!"

Tish stood next to me, taking all of it in. She motioned for me to lean down closer. She whispered, "Actually, Mom, I changed my mind. I don't want to get my ears pierced today."

"Are you sure?" I asked.

She looked over at Amma's earlobes: swollen grape tomatoes. Amma said, "C'mon, Tish! You only live once!"

Tish said, "Why does everyone say that when they're about to do dangerous things? How about 'You only live once, so don't get dead early'?"

Then she looked back at me and said, "I'm sure."

The piercer turned to Tish and said, "Your turn, honey."

I waited for Tish to speak. She said, "No, thank you. I'm not ready today."

The piercer said, "Oh, c'mon! You can do it! Be brave! Look how brave your little sister was!"

Tish looked at me, and I squeezed her hand as we walked away. She felt a little ashamed, and I felt a lot annoyed.

I don't think brave means what we've been saying it means.

We tell our children that brave means *feeling afraid and doing it anyway,* but is this the definition we want them to carry as they grow older?

When she is seventeen, headed out in a car driven by her teenage buddy, saying she's going to the movies but actually going to that kegger down the street, imagine calling to her, "Bye, babe! Be brave tonight! What I mean by that is: If you're in a scary situation, and you feel afraid to do what your friends are encouraging you to do—I want you to ignore that fear and do it anyway! Just plow right through that gut instinct of yours!"

No. That is not the understanding of brave I want my children to have. I do not want my children to become people who abandon themselves to please the crowd.

Brave does not mean feeling afraid and doing it anyway.

Brave means living from the inside out. Brave means, in every uncertain moment, turning inward, feeling for the Knowing, and speaking it out loud.

Since the Knowing is specific, personal, and ever changing, so is brave. Whether you are brave or not cannot be judged by people on the outside. Sometimes being brave requires letting the crowd think you're a coward. Sometimes being brave means letting everyone down but yourself. Amma's brave is often: loud and go for it. Tish's brave is often: quiet and wait for it. They are both brave girls, because each is true to herself. They are not divided between what they feel and know on the inside and what they say and do on the outside. Their selves are integrated. They have integrity.

Tish showed tremendous bravery that day because keeping her integrity required her to resist the pressure of the crowd.

She trusted her own voice more than she trusted the voices of others. Brave is not asking the crowd what is brave. Brave is deciding for oneself.

On the way home from the mall I said, "Tish, I know that lady made you feel unbrave today. People have different ideas about what's brave. You did the brave thing, because the brave thing is doing what your Knowing tells you to do. You don't ask others what's brave, you feel and know what's brave. What you know to do might be the opposite of what others are telling you to do. It takes special bravery to honor yourself when the crowd is pressuring you not to. It's easier just to give in. You didn't give in to the crowd today. You stood strong in what you felt and knew. To me, that's the greatest bravery. That's true confidence, which means *loyalty to self.* That's what you move through the world with, Tish: confidence. Regardless of what others are calling 'brave' at the moment: You stay loyal to yourself.

"If you keep living with confidence, the rest of your life will unfold exactly as it is meant to. It won't always be comfortable. Some will recognize your brave; others won't. Some will understand and like you; others won't. But the way others respond to your confidence is not your business. Your business is to stay loyal to you. That way, you will always know that those who do like and love you are really your people. You'll never be forced to hide or act in order to keep people if you don't hide or act to get them."

To be brave is to forsake all others to be true to yourself.

That is the vow of a confident girl.

terms

I met Liz at an airport. We were speaking at the same event somewhere out west. I flew all night to get there and then found myself in a small terminal, standing outside a circle made up of other speakers waiting to be picked up and delivered to the event. I hate how people stand in circles. I wish we'd all agree to stand around in horseshoes, with room available for awkward outsiders to join.

A woman walked over from baggage claim and stood next to me. I smiled and stayed quiet, which is my strategy for making it through. She smiled back, but her smile was different from mine. My smile says: *Hello, I am warm, polite, and unavailable.* I smile like a period. Liz smiles slowly and openly, like a question mark.

"Hi. I'm Liz."

"I know," I said. "I adore your work. I'm Glennon."

"Oh my gosh! I know you. I adore your work, too. Where are you from?"

"I live in Naples, Florida."

"What's it like to live there?"

"It's slow. It's a retirement city. I'd say the average age in my neighborhood is eighty. The cool thing is that most of my friends are turning forty and worried about starting to look old. Not me. I feel fantastic. Like a spring chicken. I go to the gym, look around at all the grandparents, and think 'Actually, I don't need to work out after all. I look amazing.' It's all perspective, right? I tell my friends to skip the Botox and just move to Naples."

Liz says, "Wonderful. How did you end up there?"

"I got neurological Lyme disease a few years ago. My entire body shut down, and I was in bed for two years and popping fifty pills a day. I went to stay in my friend's place in Naples, and I felt so much better. I moved there temporarily, and I was able to ditch the pills, so I just stayed. I've always known I wanted to live by the beach. I guess women have to almost die before we give ourselves permission to live how we want."

Liz put her hand on my arm and said, "Wait. Wow. That last thing you said—about having to almost die—can you say that again?"

I said, "I don't think so. I'm a little nervous. I have no idea what I just said."

She smiled and said, "I like you."

"I like you, too."

The next night, along with everyone else at the convention, I went to see Liz speak. I got to the event early and claimed a seat in the front but off to the side—close enough to see her clearly but not close enough for her to see me clearly. She was standing behind the podium wearing a black shirt with a high white collar, and she reminded me of a priest at a pulpit. When she started speaking, I found myself holding my breath. She spoke with gentleness and authority. A man in the front row kept talking to the woman beside him, and Liz paused midsentence, turned to him, and asked him to stop talking. He did. Something about the way she spoke, the way she carried herself, made my heart beat quicker than usual. She seemed certain, steady, free, relaxed. She was not complying and she was not rebelling. She was creating something new. She was *original*. I wanted to ask "Can you say all of that again?"

The next night, all the speakers attended a fancy banquet in a ski lodge at the top of a mountain. Snow was flurrying outside the floor-to-ceiling windows, and people were flurrying inside, trying to figure out where to stand and who was important enough to talk to.

I saw Liz in a corner across the room, surrounded. My general policy is to honor people I admire by leaving them alone. I didn't that night. I walked over to her, and when she saw me she smiled like another beginning. I drew closer, joined the huddle. The entire circle was pressing Liz with questions and requests for advice like she was a vending machine. I wanted to step on their toes.

After a while, the host of the event walked over and said to Liz, "It's time to take our seats for dinner. May I lead you to your table?"

Liz pointed to me and asked, "Can I sit with my friend?"

The woman looked nervous, then apologetic. "I'm sorry. We've promised the donors that you'd sit with them."

"Okay," she said. She looked forlorn. She squeezed my arm and said, "I'll miss you."

During the dinner I thought about how much I liked Liz and how sad it was that we wouldn't actually be able to be friends. Attempting to be her friend would be like intentionally writing a bad check. I am not a good friend. I have never been capable of or willing to commit to the maintenance that the rules of friendship dictate. I cannot remember birthdays. I do not want to meet for coffee. I will not host the baby shower.

I won't text back because it's an eternal game of Ping-Pong, the texting. It never ends. I inevitably disappoint friends, so after enough of that, I decided I would stop trying. I don't want to live in constant debt. This is okay with me. I have a sister and children and a dog. One cannot have it all.

A few weeks after the event, Liz sent me an email saying she thought we should try friendship. She sent along this poem:

I honor your gods,
I drink at your well,
I bring an undefended heart to our meeting place.
I have no cherished outcomes,
I will not negotiate by withholding,
I am not subject to disappointment.

She offered a new friendship memo: that for us there would be no arbitrary rules, obligations, or expectations. We would not owe each other anything other than admiration, respect, love—and that was all done already. We became friends.

A while later, I invited Liz to come stay with me. It was shortly after I'd met Abby, and I was walking through my days stunned. I was deeply in love for the first time in my life, and I had told no one except my sister about any of it. Liz and I stayed up late that first night, talking about everything but my desperate heart and aching body and muddled mind.

The next morning, my alarm rang at 5:30, which didn't matter because I didn't sleep anymore. I rolled over and tiptoed to the kitchen so I wouldn't wake Liz upstairs. I took my coffee outside and stood in my backyard. It was still dark and cold, but the pink-tinged horizon hinted at the coming sun. I stood there, stared at the sky, and, as I'd done each day since I'd met Abby, I thought: *Help, please.*

In that moment, I was reminded of a story about a woman

who had become stranded on top of an icy mountain. She frantically prayed that God would rescue her before she froze to death. She called to the heavens, "If you exist, God, send help!"

A little while later, a helicopter circled above and dropped a ladder.

"No," the woman said. "Go away! I'm waiting for God!"

Then a park ranger walked by and asked, "Need some help, sister?"

"No! Go away! I'm waiting for God!"

The woman froze to death. She showed up at the gates of heaven—pissed—and demanded, "WHY, GOD? Why did you let me die?"

God said, "Honey. I sent a helicopter. I sent a park ranger. What the hell were you waiting for?"

I thought: *I am freezing to death while Liz Freakin' Gilbert, a friend I admire, trust, and love—who happens to also be a world-renowned spiritual teacher—is asleep upstairs. Maybe Liz is my park ranger.*

When she woke up, Liz found me at the bottom of the stairs in my pajamas, teary, desperate, humbled.

I said, "I need you."

She said, "Okay, Honeyhead."

We sat down on my couch, and I spilled it all. I told her about how Abby and I had met, how we'd spent the past weeks falling deeper in love through emails, how our letters felt like blood transfusions. Each one I read and wrote pumped fresh life through my veins. I told her how ridiculous and impossible it all was. It was thrilling and terrifying to hear the words fall out of my mouth, like I was crossing some point of no return. I was expecting her to be shocked. She was not shocked. Her eyes were sparkly, lovingly amused, soft, smiling. She looked relieved somehow.

I said, "It will never work out."

She said, "Maybe not. Maybe she's just an Abby-shaped door inviting you to leave what's not true enough anymore."

I said, "It will ruin Craig."

She said, "There is no such thing as one-way liberation, honey."

I said, "Can you imagine the havoc this would wreak on my parents, on my friends, on my career?"

She said, "Yes, everyone you love would be uncomfortable for a long while, maybe. What is better: uncomfortable truth or comfortable lies? Every truth is a kindness, even if it makes others uncomfortable. Every untruth is an unkindness, even if it makes others comfortable."

I said, "I barely know her."

She said, "But you do know yourself."

I said, "What if I leave for her and this isn't even real?"

She looked at me. She did not say anything.

We sat together in the quiet. She held my hand, lightly, lovingly.

I said, "I am real. What I feel and want and know. That's all real."

"Yes," Liz said. "You are real."

It is a blessing to know a free woman. Sometimes she will stop by and hold up a mirror for you. She will help you remember who you are.

erikas

Recently, my friend Erika called my cell phone. I will never understand why people insist upon calling my cell phone. It's such an aggressive action to take: *calling* someone. Each time my phone rings, I have a heart attack like my pocket's on fire and a tiny siren is going off.

I'd also like to take this opportunity to address texting. Texting = Better Than Calling. *Unless.*

Unless you are one of those people who doles out texts like IOUs. Unless you believe that whenever you feel like it, you can just poke at me, ping me, jump into my day like *Hiiiiii* and feel so entitled to a response that the next time I see you, you will arrange your face in an injured manner and say quietly, "Hey. You doing okay? I just never heard back . . ." At this moment, I have 183 unread texts. Texts are not the boss of me, and neither is anybody who texts me. I have decided, once and for all, that just because someone texts me does not obligate me to respond. If I believed differently, I'd walk around all day feeling anxious and indebted, responding instead of creating.

Now that we've established why I have no friends, let's return to Erika.

Erika and I went to college together. She was a born artist, but studied business because her mother was a corporate executive and wanted Erika to become one, too. Erika resented every minute she spent in those business classes. It's nearly impossible to blaze one's own path while following in someone else's footsteps.

Erika returned to our dorm each day and recovered from her business boredom by painting. She graduated with a business degree, then fell in love with a fantastic guy and worked in a corporate office to put him through medical school. Next, the babies came, and she quit her job to stay home and care for them. All the while, she heard a voice nagging her to start painting again. One day, she told me she planned to honor that longing—to honor herself—by enrolling in art school. I heard fizz and fire in her voice for the first time in a decade.

So I answered the phone in celebration of Erika's commitment and I said, "Hey! How is school going?"

She was quiet for a moment and then said, "Oh that. That was silly. Brett is so busy, and the kids need me. Art school just seemed so selfish after a while."

Why do women find it honorable to dismiss ourselves?
Why do we decide that denying our longing is the responsible thing to do?
Why do we believe that what will thrill and fulfill us will hurt our people?
Why do we mistrust ourselves so completely?

Here's why: Because our culture was built upon and benefits from the control of women. The way power justifies controlling a group is by conditioning the masses to believe that the group cannot be trusted. So the campaign to convince us to mistrust women begins early and comes from everywhere.

When we are little girls, our families, teachers, and peers insist that our loud voices, bold opinions, and strong feelings are "too much" and unladylike, so we learn to not trust our personalities.

Childhood stories promise us that girls who dare to leave the path or explore get attacked by big bad wolves and pricked by deadly spindles, so we learn to not trust our curiosity.

The beauty industry convinces us that our thighs, frizz, skin, fingernails, lips, eyelashes, leg hair, and wrinkles are repulsive and must be covered and manipulated, so we learn to not trust the bodies we live in.

Diet culture promises us that controlling our appetite is the key to our worthiness, so we learn to not trust our own hunger.

Politicians insist that our judgment about our bodies and futures cannot be trusted, so our own reproductive systems must be controlled by lawmakers we don't know in places we've never been.

The legal system proves to us again and again that even our own memories and experiences will not be trusted. If twenty women come forward and say, "He did it," and he says, "No, I didn't," they will believe him while discounting and maligning us every damn time.

And religion, *sweet Jesus*. The lesson of Adam and Eve—the first formative story I was told about God and a woman—was this: When a woman wants more, she defies God, betrays her partner, curses her family, and destroys the world.

We weren't born distrusting and fearing ourselves. That was part of our taming. We were taught to believe that who we are in our natural state is bad and dangerous. They convinced us to be afraid of ourselves. So we do not honor our own bodies, curiosity, hunger, judgment, experience, or ambition. Instead, we lock away our true selves. Women who are best at this disappearing act earn the highest praise: *She is so selfless.*

Can you imagine? The epitome of womanhood is to lose one's self completely.

That is the end goal of every patriarchal culture. Because a very effective way to control women is to convince women to control themselves.

I tried to control myself for so long.

I spent thirty years covering and injecting my face with potions and poison trying to fix my skin. Then I quit. And my skin was good.

For twenty years, I was attached to a hair dryer and straightener trying to tame my curls. Then I quit. And my hair was good.

I binged and purged and dieted for decades trying to control my body. When I quit, my body became what it was always meant to become. And it was good, too.

I numbed myself with food and booze trying to control my anger. When I quit, I learned that my anger never meant that there was something wrong with me. It meant that there was something wrong. *Out there.* Something I might have the power to change. I stopped being a quiet peacekeeper and started being a loud peacemaker. My anger was good.

I had been deceived. The only thing that was ever wrong with me was my belief that there was something wrong with me. I quit spending my life trying to control myself and began to trust myself. We only control what we don't trust. We can either control our selves or love our selves, but we can't do both. Love is the opposite of control. Love demands trust.

I love myself now. Self-love means that I have a relationship with myself built on trust and loyalty. I trust myself to have my own back, so my allegiance is to the voice within. I'll abandon everyone else's expectations of me before I'll abandon myself. I'll disappoint everyone else before I'll disappoint myself. I'll forsake all others before I'll forsake myself. Me and myself: *We are till death do us part.*

What the world needs is more women who have quit fearing themselves and started trusting themselves.

What the world needs is masses of women who are entirely out of control.

beach houses

I wrote to my community recently: *Do with your Self whatever it is you want to do. You can trust your Self.* Someone responded,

> Isn't it irresponsible to suggest that we should do whatever we want to do? Most nights, by the time I get home I want to drink an entire bottle of Malibu. Pretty sure I shouldn't trust all of my desires.

I have a friend who has struggled mightily with money for decades. She recently told me that she was *this close* to renting an expensive beach house even though she was deep in debt. She knew from her roots that she couldn't trust this desire of hers, but she wanted this vacation for her family so badly that she was prepared to allow her desire to override her Knowing.

When I asked why she was so desperate for this house, she

looked down at her hands and said, "I see all the pictures on social media of families at the shore. They're relaxing together. They're off their damn phones and just being together. My family is so disconnected right now. The kids are growing so fast. Tom and I never really talk anymore. I feel like we're losing each other. I want to slow down. I want to talk to my kids and husband more. I want to know what's going on in their lives. I want to have fun together again."

Instead of renting the beach house, my friend bought a two-dollar basket and placed it on a table in her foyer. She asked her husband and teenagers to leave their phones in the basket for an hour each weeknight. Her family began preparing, eating, and cleaning up after dinner together. There was a lot of grumbling about this new system at first, but then came the laughter, talking, and connection she'd yearned for. Her basket turned out to be a two-dollar beach house.

So, that woman's nightly desire for a bottle of Malibu? That was just a surface desire. I know this because her Knowing didn't trust it. A surface desire is one that conflicts with our Knowing. We must ask of our surface desires: *What is the desire beneath this desire? Is it rest? Is it peace?*

Our deep desires are wise, true, beautiful, and things we can grant ourselves without abandoning our Knowing. Following our deep desire always returns us to integrity. If your desire feels wrong to you: Go deeper. You can trust yourself. You just have to get low enough.

I have spent the last decade of my life listening to women talk about what they most desire. This is what women tell me they want:

I want a minute to take a deep breath.
I want rest, peace, passion.

I want good food and true, wild, intimate sex.
I want relationships with no lies.
I want to be comfortable in my own skin.
I want to be seen, to be loved.
I want joy and safety for my children and for everyone else's
children.
I want justice for all.
I want help, community, and connection.
I want to be forgiven, and I want to finally forgive.
I want enough money and power to stop feeling afraid.
I want to find my purpose down here and live it out fully.
I want to look at the news and see less pain, more love.
I want to look at the people in my life and really see them and love
them.
I want to look in the mirror and really see myself and love myself.
I want to feel alive.

The blueprints of heaven are etched in the deep desires of women. What women want is good. What women want is beautiful. And what women want *is* dangerous, but not to women. Not to the common good. What women want is a threat to the injustice of the status quo. If we unlocked and unleashed ourselves:

Imbalanced relationships would be equalized.
Children would be fed.
Corrupt governments would topple.
Wars would end.
Civilizations would be transformed.

If women trusted and claimed their desires, the world as we know it would crumble. Perhaps that is precisely what needs to happen so we can rebuild truer, more beautiful lives, relationships, families, and nations in their place.

Maybe Eve was never meant to be our warning. Maybe she was meant to be our model.

Own your wanting.

Eat the apple.

Let it burn.

temperatures

One morning, I called my friend Martha and began telling her all the reasons I could not leave my marriage. Then I began sharing all the reasons I could not stay in my marriage. I kept talking, talking, talking, weighing every angle, arguing myself into corners and then around and around in circles.

Eventually she said, "Glennon, stop. You are in your head. The answers you need this time aren't in there. They're in your body. Try dropping into your body. Right now on the phone. Drop lower."

This was becoming a theme in my life, all this sinking and dropping.

She asked, "You in there yet?"

"I think so," I said.

"Okay, now consider both decisions. Inhabit yourself and feel. Does saying good-bye to Abby feel warm to you?"

"No. That feels cold, actually. It feels icy. It makes me feel like I'll die of cold."

"Now consider being with Abby. How does that feel?"

"It feels warm. Soft. Spacious."

"Okay, Glennon. Your body is nature, and nature is pure. I know that's hard for you to accept because you have been at war with your body for so long. You think your body is bad, but it is not. It's wise. Your body will tell you things your mind will talk you out of. Your body is telling you what direction life is in. Try trusting it. Turn away from what feels cold. Go toward what feels warm."

Now when I sense danger, I believe the cold and leave. When I sense joy, I believe the warm and stay.

These days, in business meetings, when I request an explanation for a decision someone has made, the women on my team know that I'm not looking for justifications, judgments, or opinions. I'm looking for Knowing. So the decision maker will say, "I did the research and sat with these options for a while. This option felt warm to me. The alternative felt cold." That will be the end of the discussion. I trust women who trust themselves.

mirrors

For a long while I pretended not to know that even though I had only one life, I was spending it inside a lonely marriage.

When the Knowing threatened to rise, I'd shove it back down. There was no point in admitting I knew what I knew, because I would never do what the Knowing would require me to do. I would never leave my children's father. I'd just pretend not to know forever. I was a mother, and I had responsibilities.

In middle school we learned about parenting by caring for an egg. In order to pass the unit, we had to return the uncracked egg to the teacher at the end of the week. Those who left their egg home in the dark all week fared best; some of their eggs went rotten, but that didn't matter as long as they remained uncracked.

I parented Tish like she was an egg. I'd say, "She is so sensitive, so fragile." I worried about her and counted that as love. I protected her and counted that as mothering. I'd have kept her at home in the dark forever if I could have. She and I were living in a story I had written, and I was the hero. I would never let her crack, and I would pass parenting.

I am drinking coffee on Tish's bed, watching her get ready for school. She is brushing her yards of Rapunzel hair.

I watch her look at herself in the mirror and then back at me. She says, "My hair is too babyish. Can I cut it like yours?"

I look at the two of us in that mirror. Right there in front of me, I can finally see that Tish is not an egg. She is a girl, becoming a woman.

Every time she looks at me, she is seeing herself, too. And she is asking:

Mom, how does a woman wear her hair?
Mom, how does a woman love and be loved?
Mom, how does a woman live?

Tish asks, "Will you put my hair up in a pony, Mom?"

I walk into the bathroom, find a ponytail holder, come back, and stand behind her. I have pulled her hair up a thousand times, but all of a sudden, she's too tall. I can't even see the top of her head. She has grown at least an inch overnight. When she was a baby, every day felt like a year. Now every morning, another inch.

I look at Tish and I think:

I am staying in this marriage for my little girl.

But would I want this marriage for my little girl?

eyes

When Craig and I moved to our home in Naples, we bought a gigantic silver mirror that we found on clearance. We never got around to hanging it. We just leaned it against our bedroom wall and hoped the leaning looked purposeful and artsy.

The day my therapist insisted that my feelings weren't real, I decided to say good-bye to Abby and remain in my marriage. She was the expert, and she was right. Good mothers don't break their children's hearts in order to follow their own.

I sat on my bedroom carpet cross-legged, looking directly into my own eyes in that mirror.

It's important to take a good look at yourself every once in a while. Not the way you look at yourself while you're getting dressed or putting on makeup. Not the way you look at your thighs or sunspots or chin hairs. Not that way. I mean you need to look dead into your own eyes—at your real self. You need to make sure there are no lies there. You need to make sure the eyes in the mirror are the eyes of a woman you respect.

As I looked deep into my own eyes, the woman in the mirror and I had a reckoning.

I asked myself: *Is the decision to continue abandoning yourself really what your children need from you?*

Mothers have martyred themselves in their children's names since the beginning of time. We have lived as if she who disappears the most, loves the most. We have been conditioned to prove our love by slowly ceasing to exist.

What a terrible burden for children to bear—to know that they are the reason their mother stopped living. What a terrible burden for our daughters to bear—to know that if they choose to become mothers, this will be their fate, too. Because if we show them that being a martyr is the highest form of love, that is what they will become. They will feel obligated to love as well as their mothers loved, after all. They will believe they have permission to live only as fully as their mothers allowed themselves to live.

If we keep passing down the legacy of martyrdom to our daughters, with whom does it end? Which woman ever gets to live? And when does the death sentence begin? At the wedding altar? In the delivery room? Whose delivery room—our children's or our own? When we call martyrdom love we teach our children that when love begins, life ends. This is why Jung suggested: *There is no greater burden on a child than the unlived life of a parent.*

What if love is not the process of disappearing for the beloved but of *emerging* for the beloved? What if a mother's responsibility is teaching her children that love does not lock the lover away but *frees* her? What if a responsible mother is not one who shows her children how to slowly die but how to stay wildly alive until the day she dies? What if the call of motherhood is not to be a martyr but to be a *model*?

Right there, on the floor, I looked deep into my own eyes. I let the Knowing rise and stay.

My children do not need me to save them.

My children need to watch me save myself.

I'd quit using my children as an excuse to not be brave and start seeing them as my reason to be brave. I would leave their father and I would claim friendship-and-fire love, or I would be alone. But I would never again be alone in a relationship and pretend that was love. I would never again settle for a relationship or life less beautiful than the one I'd want for my child.

I'd divorce Craig. Because I am a mother. And I have responsibilities.

I stood up off the carpet and called Abby. We had not seen each other since the night we met in Chicago.

I said, "I'm in love with you. I'm leaving Craig. I'm telling him today."

She said, "Glennon. Oh my God. I am so in love with you. I'm so happy right now. And I'm so afraid for you. Are you sure you're ready to do this? We've never even touched."

I said, "I know. But I'm not leaving just because of you. I'm leaving because now that I know this kind of love exists, I can't pretend it doesn't anymore. I can't unknow what I know, and I can't unbecome who I am now. So I'm leaving—not just because I love you but because I love this version of me. The one that woke up when we met. I have to either leave him or myself. I'm going to leave him. Now that I know this, I have to tell him that I know. I don't owe Craig the rest of my life, but I do owe him my honesty. It'll be hard, but it'll finally be the right kind of hard."

That afternoon I sat down with Craig and I said—with tenderness but without apology—that I was leaving. I said, "Our marriage is complete. We have been the healing partners we were meant to be for each other. Our marriage has been a great success. And now it's done. I'm in love with Abby. As soon as I knew, I needed you to know, too."

He was very quiet, and after a long while he said, "Three years ago, you gave me more grace than I deserved. Now I'm going to return it to you. I want you to be happy."

We didn't stay in that place. The next few months were a roller coaster. But we kept coming back to: Grace for you. Grace for me.

Later, when he was ready, we sat down to tell the kids. I've hurt many people I love in my life, but that was the worst of it. I looked directly into my babies' terrified faces and said, "I am about to break your hearts. Over time we will rebuild our hearts, and they will be bigger and stronger. But for now, it's just going to hurt. Sometimes we have to do hard things because they are true things. Your dad and I want you to live the truth of who you are even when it's hard and scary and painful. I am about to show you how that's done."

They cried. The news changed them, right there on that couch. I saw it happen. We held one another while we let so much burn. Craig told them, "It's going to be okay. Abby is a good woman. We are going to be a new kind of family, but we are still going to be a beautiful family."

He gave our children permission to love Abby, which was the greatest gift he's ever given me. Maybe the greatest gift anyone has ever given me.

We told our families.

We told our friends.

All of that happened within two weeks.

Forty years, five months, and two weeks.

gardens

I learned how to be desirable very young. I learned how to match myself to the women on television. I learned how to highlight my hair, curl my eyelashes, wear jeans that made my ass look right, and stay thin by any means necessary. I knew how to become a billboard for myself, and after a boy had chosen me, I knew what to do next. I knew what kind of panties to be wearing and how to arch my back just so and how to make the right noises at the right time. I knew what sounds and moves would make him desire me even more and make him think I desired him. Sex was a stage and I was the player.

I knew how to be desired.

I did not know desire.

I knew how to be wanted.

I did not know want.

Until I met her.

After I told Craig our marriage was over, Abby flew to LA to be honored at an awards show. She was receiving an Icon Award from ESPN to celebrate her soccer career and retirement. It was an ending for her. I wanted to be there, as her beginning. "I'm coming," I said.

We had not seen each other since the night we'd first met. We had never been alone together. We had never touched, except for the moment I'd grabbed her arm and quickly recoiled to stop the electricity. In the past month, we'd both let our lives burn for the chance to be together. More to the point, we set our lives on fire for the chance to become the women we were born to be.

The morning of my flight, I woke while it was still dark and prepared two bags: one to check and the other to carry on. In my carry-on, I packed makeup, a hair straightener, heels, and a white dress. I drove to the airport, suspended between an old version of myself and one I didn't know yet. When the plane took off, I tried to read. Then I tried to watch television, but I couldn't focus on either one. One thought was on a loop in my mind: *You will be alone with Abby in a matter of hours, and you have never even kissed a girl before.* I remember being especially afraid of the eye contact. I had never made eye contact while being intimate. I'd once told Abby that, and she had been shocked and sad. At the end of that conversation, she had said, "If we ever get to touch each other, please know that I will not let your eyes look away from mine." I did not know if I was capable.

Halfway through the flight, I pulled my bag out from under my seat and walked to the airplane bathroom. I took off my sweatpants and sweatshirt, pulled on my dress and heels, applied my makeup, and straightened my hair. When I sat back down, the woman next to me looked over and asked, "If I go in that bathroom, will that happen to me?"

As the plane landed at LAX, my first thought was: *Oh my God, we are finally in the same city.* I took a cab to the hotel. When the cab pulled up, I texted, "I'm here." Abby typed back, "Room 1140." I put the phone away. I got into the elevator, pressed the buttons, then stepped out onto floor 11. I walked through the hallway and stopped in front of her room. There was a note taped to the door that said, "Come in."

I breathed deep, fussed with my hair, shot a quick prayer up: *Please be here with us.*

I knocked softly and then opened the door.

Abby was leaning against the desk across the room with one leg propped up on a chair, barefoot. She was wearing a charcoal T-shirt, sky-blue jeans, and a necklace that looked like dog tags.

My first thought: There she is. That's my person.

She'd later tell me that her first thought had been: There she is. That's my wife.

She smiled. It was not a casual smile. It was a smile that said: *There you are and here we are, finally.* She stood up and walked toward me. I let the door shut behind me, my bags still out in the hallway. She wrapped her arms around me. We melted, my head into her chest, her heart beating through her T-shirt onto my skin. She was shaking and I was shaking, and we both, for a long while, stood there and breathed each other in and held each other and shook together.

Then she pulled away and looked into my eyes. That was the moment we locked.

Then

The kiss.

The wall.

The bed.

White dress on the floor.

Naked, unafraid.

The original plan.

On Earth as it is in heaven.

I never looked away from her. Not once.

The longer we've been together, the more naked and un-afraid I've become. I don't act anymore. I just want.

VOWS

Fifteen years ago, when I got pregnant with my second child, I decided to wait to find out the biological sex of the baby.

I learned the sex of my firstborn before his birth, but now I was a parenting veteran, so I was vastly more mature and disciplined. At what would have been the reveal sonogram, I lay on the examination table and looked back and forth between the small green screen and the technician's face. Both were indecipherable. When the technician left and the doctor arrived, I had to trust what she told me—that there was, in fact, a human being inside me and that this being seemed, in her words, "Fine, so far."

A *fine, so far* human being was exactly what I'd been hoping for. A *fine, so far* human being is what I have continued hoping for throughout my parenting career.

With that news—and only that news—I left the doctor's office. When I got home, I sat on the family room couch, stared at the wall, and thought about how far I'd come from the controlling, dramatic, first-time mother I used to be.

Look at me, I thought, *patiently letting the universe unfold as it should.*

Then I picked up the phone and called the doctor's office. When the receptionist answered I said, "Hello. This is Glennon. I was just there."

"Oh. Did you leave something here?"

"Yes. I left extremely important information there. Let's just say, hypothetically, that I changed my mind. Could I still find out the sex of my baby?"

She said, "Hold on, please."

I held on please. She came back and said, "It's a girl. You're having a girl."

One of my favorite words is *selah*.

Selah is found in the Hebrew Bible seventy-four times. Scholars believe that when it appears in the text, it is a direction to the reader to stop reading and be still for a moment, because the previous idea is important enough to consider deeply. The poetry in scripture is meant to transform, and the scribes knew that change begins through reading but can be completed only in quiet contemplation. *Selah* appears in Hebrew music, too. It's believed to be a signal to the music director to silence the choir for a long moment, to hold space between notes. The silence, of course, is when the music sinks in.

Selah is the holy silence when the recipient of transformational words, music, and sketchily acquired information from radiology receptionists pauses long enough to be changed forever.

Selah is the nothingness just before the big bang of a woman exploding into a new universe.

You're having a girl. My eyes widened like a camera lens adjusting to a blast of light. I sat on the couch, phone still in hand, wordless, motionless.

"Thank you," I finally said to the receptionist. "Thank you. I love you. Bye."

I hung up and called my sister.

"Sister, we're having a girl. We are having a *girl*."

"Wait," she said. "*What?* How did you find out? Did they accidentally tell you?"

"Yes. After I accidentally asked."

She said, "Holy shit. This is the best day of our lives. Another one of us. We are going to have a third. A third sister."

"I know. Do not ever tell Craig that I called you first."

"Obviously," she said.

Just then I heard my two-year-old son, Chase, waking up from his nap, hollering from his crib his usual announcement, "I AWAKE GWENNON!"

I hung up, climbed the stairs, and opened Chase's door. He sat up in bed and smiled. For the first time I saw him as my daughter's big brother. She's so lucky, I thought. I kissed his silk cheeks, and he followed me downstairs, holding the railing, one careful step at a time. I wrapped him up in a puffy jacket, scarf, and hat and took him for a walk on the path around the tiny pond in our neighborhood. I needed to get outside. I needed more space surrounding this gigantic news. I needed sky.

I remember that Chase and I were chilly. I remember that the air was crisp and the sky was clear. I remember that halfway around the pond, when our little town house had become tiny in the distance, a goose crossed the path in front of us and Chase laughed. I remember that the goose got a little too close, so I picked up Chase and I walked the rest of the way around the pond with him in my arms, his legs wrapped around my waist,

my nose nestled in his neck. All these years later, I can still smell
his neck: powder and toddler sweat. I can still remember thinking: *I'm carrying both of my children. All by myself. My son's head
resting on my shoulder, my daughter's heart beating in my body. I have
everything.*

We decided to name our daughter Patricia, after my mother.
We'd call her Tish. She'd be wrapped in the same olive skin,
black hair, and Japanese features her older brother inherited
from his dad. I dreamt of her all day, every day. I could not
wait for Tish to be born. In fact, when I was thirty-eight weeks
pregnant, I got in the bathtub and told Craig that I would not
come out until he found a way to schedule an induction. He
found a way. A few days later, I was holding my daughter.
When the nurse placed her in my arms, I whispered, "Hi,
angel"—and then took a good look at her. I was surprised. She
was pink, with light skin, hair, eyes. She and I matched.

Along with his looks, Tish's older brother inherited his father's easy-breezy, accommodating temperament. I'd made the
rookie mistake of attributing Chase's easiness to my masterful
parenting. When my friends complained about how hard parenting was, I'd agree outwardly and think: *Suckers. What's so
hard about this?* Then Tish was born, and I suddenly understood
what was so hard about this.

Tish was born *concerned*. As an infant, she cried constantly.
As a toddler, her default was set at displeased. For the first few
years of her life, I spent all day, every day, trying to make her
happy. By the time she was six, I'd given up on happy. Each
morning, I'd sit on the floor outside her bedroom door holding
a whiteboard that said, "Good morning, Tish! We will be pleasant today!" When she came out scowling, I'd point to the board
and explain that "pleasant" meant: *Act* happy. Just pretend.
This is our social contract with the world, kid: ACT HAPPY.
Suffer silently like the rest of us, for the love of God.

Tish rejected my memo. She would not act. She refused to be pleasant. One day when Craig came home from work, I met him at the door, crying. Tish was upstairs, crying. I said to him, "She is untenable. Incorrigible. I cannot handle her. Where did this drama COME FROM?" To his credit, he did not answer in words. He just looked at me sitting on the floor, weeping, and gave me enough time to think: *Oh. I see. Tish is me.*

My therapist neighbor warns me not to force this limiting, narcissistic narrative on my daughter; she insists that children are not carbon copies of their parents. To that I say, "Okay. I see your point. But I also see my daughter, lady."

When I realized that Tish was me, I remembered that *acting happy* was what had almost killed me. I quit trying to make Tish happy or pleasant and decided just to help her be Tish. Tish is fourteen now. She is still turned inside out. What she feels and thinks on the inside, the world hears and sees on the outside. When she becomes upset, we assume she has her own valid reason. So we say, "I see that you're upset. Are you ready for a solution yet? Or do you just need to feel this way for a while?" She usually just needs to feel this way for a while, because she is becoming. We don't rush her anymore. In fact, when we try to rush through life, through pain, through beauty, Tish slows us down and points. She shows us what we need to notice, think, and feel in order to stay human. She is the kindest, wisest, most honest person I know. There is no one walking the Earth I respect more. Tish is our family's conscience and prophet. She is our *selah*.

When her father and I divorced, Tish's world fell apart. Day in and day out, week after week, month after month, she held us close to the pain. When the rest of us just wanted to "get over it," to act happy, Tish kept us honest. She would not act. She would not be pleasant. She insisted that when worlds crumble, it is time to stop the world for a while. She let us skip nothing, and she made us feel everything. She asked the hardest questions. She cried herself to sleep every night for a very long time. She was our Joan of Arc, marching us straight into battle, day in and day out.

For her, war was being waged on two fronts. The first was the divorce between her parents. But the second family transformation rocked her just as deeply: watching me fall in love. Tish had always understood that she and her siblings were the loves of my life. Her father and I were partners—in love with the family we'd created but not with each other. She was watching her mother, who until now had existed solely to serve and adore her, become fully human in front of her eyes. She lost her mother as she knew her. She watched me become a whole, alive woman. She watched me become complicated. Things had seemed so simple for so long. As I fell in love with Abby, Tish felt as though I was falling away from her.

One night, as the battle raged on, I was tucking Tish into bed. Since she knows her feelings and how to speak them clear as crystal, she looked up at me and said, "Mommy. I am afraid that I'm going to lose you."

I sat down on the bed and said, "Oh, baby. You are never going to lose me. You are never going to lose me, baby."

"Say it again," she whispered.

So I said it again. And again. I never stopped saying it. Three years later, this is still our nightly ritual.

Lights out. "You're never gonna lose me, baby."

This means that the last thing I say to my prophet daughter every single night is a bold-faced lie. In this life of unknowables, there is one thing I know for sure, and that is that some-day my girl is going to lose me.

I used to lie to Tish all the time. I used to promise her things that would temporarily dazzle her, placate her, protect her.

Yes, I'm certain that heaven is real. Yes, I believe in Santa! No, your parents will never, ever get divorced. Yes, life is fair and there are good guys and bad guys. Mommy knows best. Everything happens for a reason. You are safe, honey. I will keep you safe.

That was back when I thought my job was to keep Tish safe instead of allowing her to become brave. Back when I thought I should make Tish's life easy instead of allowing her to learn that she can handle life's hard. Back when I thought there was more magic in what was pretend than what was real. Back when I believed a mother was supposed to be her daughter's hero instead of allowing her daughter to become her own hero.

I thought my role was to protect Tish from pain, so I ended up teaching her that disaster was just around the corner. By shielding her constantly, I taught her how to be afraid. I taught her to hide. I taught her that she was not capable of handling what life might bring. *Be careful, baby, be careful, baby, come here, honey. Mommy will protect you.*

But then, four years ago, I became the very one who brought disaster to her and placed it right in her lap.

I broke the heart I had been given to protect.

I watched Tish grieve, and then I watched her rise.

I learned that you can break a child's heart without break-ing a child. Now, three years after the divorce, Tish is no lon-ger in hiding, on constant lookout for danger up ahead. The worst came, and she survived. She is a little girl who no longer has to avoid the fires of life, because she has learned that she is fireproof. Only people who stand in the fire can know that. That is the one thing I need my children to know about them-selves: Nothing will destroy them. So I do not want to protect them from life's fires; I want to point them toward the fire and say, "I see your fear, and it's big. I also see your courage, and it's bigger. We can do hard things, baby. We are fireproof."

If I could do it again, I'd toss out the sign I once hung on Tish's nursery wall that read: "Every Little Thing Is Gonna Be Alright." I'd replace it with Buechner's "Here is the world. Beautiful and terrible things will happen. Don't be afraid."

Since I don't believe in lying to Tish anymore, I've been brainstorming simple ways to adjust my nightly vow to her and make it true. It's been tricky. For example, I *could* tuck her in, smile at her, and say, "Lights out, honey. You're definitely gonna lose me." But that's a bridge too far, perhaps.

Here's where I've landed. Here's the promise and hope I have for Tish, for myself, for all of us:

"Good night, baby. You're never gonna lose *you*."

touch trees

I am lying on the couch, enjoying my favorite pastime, which is watching very bad television. I have been sober for eighteen years, and during that time every single one of my painkillers has been taken from me. I no longer drink, do drugs, binge and purge, snark incessantly, or even shop compulsively (often). But I can promise this: They will take Bravo and HGTV from my cold, dead hands.

An intriguing televised situation unfolds in front of me. The host of the show I am watching is a rugged, outdoorsy-type man. He has gone out into the woods by himself. He seems to have done this on purpose, so right away I understand that he is very strange. The man gets himself lost in these woods. I do not know why he didn't see this lostness coming, but he seems surprised, so I feel worried. There appears to be no rescue in sight. There appears to be *nothing* in sight, except for various animals and plants and mud and other natural things that are perhaps typical of the woods. I can't be certain because I've never been in the woods since woods are not for people.

Our Survivorman has not eaten for days. He is also out of water. My superpower is empathy, which means that I am often unable to distinguish between what is happening to other people and what is happening to me. So, when my wife walks into the family room, she finds me curled up in a ball beneath a blanket, slowly dying from malnutrition and thirst.

She raises her eyebrows. "You okay, honey?"

I say, "No. Look at this. I think he's going to die. He is lost in the woods, and he is starving. I really don't see how we're going to get out of this one."

My wife says, "Okay, babe. Remember what we talked about. How reality TV works is: If you are seeing it *here*, there has to be a camera crew *there*. Which means there's also likely a protein bar available. He is definitely going to be okay, honey."

I am grateful for this reminder, as it allows me to come out from under my blanket and watch the rest of the show with some boundaries. Boundaries are just what I need in order to take in the lesson Fraudulent Survivorman is about to teach me.

He says that when someone is lost in the woods, the main objective is to get found. The best way to get found is to stay in one place. Unfortunately, if one is lost in the woods, she *cannot* stay in one place, because she has to go out and try to find food and supplies to survive.

What I am gathering is that in order to survive, a lost person must:

1. Stay in the same place; and
2. Not stay in the same place.

Uh-huh. This is why the woods are not for people, I think. I keep listening.

Fraudulent Survivorman has a solution. He says the most effective strategy that a lost person can use to increase her likelihood of getting found and thriving is this:

She must find herself a Touch Tree.

A Touch Tree is one recognizable, strong, large tree that becomes the lost one's home base. She can adventure out into the woods as long as she returns to her Touch Tree—again and again. This perpetual returning will keep her from getting too far gone.

I've spent much of my life lost in the woods of pain, relationships, religion, career, service, success, and failure. Looking back on those times, I can trace my lostness back to a decision to make something outside myself my Touch Tree. An identity. A set of beliefs. An institution. Aspirational ideals. A job. Another person. A list of rules. Approval. An old version of myself.

Now when I feel lost, I remember that I am not the woods. I am my own tree. So I return to myself and reinhabit myself. As I do, I feel my chin rise and my body straighten.

I reach deeply into the rich soil beneath me, made up of every girl and woman I've ever been, every face I've loved, every love I've lost, every place I've been, every conversation I've had, every book I've read and song I've sung, everything, everything, crumbling and mixing and decomposing underneath. Nothing wasted. My entire past there, holding me up and feeding me now. All of this too low for anyone else to see, just there for me to draw from. Then up and up all the way to my branches, my imagination, too high for anyone else to see—reaching beyond, growing toward the light and warmth. Then the middle, the trunk, the only part of me entirely visible to the world. Pulpy and soft inside, just tough enough on the outside to protect and hold me. Exposed and safe.

I am as ancient as the earth I'm planted in and as new as my tiniest bloom. I am my own Touch Tree: strong, singular, alive. Still growing.

I have everything I need, beneath me, above me, inside me.

I am never gonna lose me.

buckets

Just as I was about to fall asleep the other night, I heard a faint knock on my bedroom door. "Come in," I said.

Tish walked into my room and stopped at my bedside watery-eyed, apologetic. "What's wrong, baby?"

"I'm scared."

"Of what?"

"Everything. But nothing. It's not that anything's wrong, really. It's just—I'm all by myself in here. In my body. I'm just . . . lonely or something. I forget during the day, when I'm busy, but at night, in bed, I remember. I'm all alone in here. It's scary."

Tish climbed into my bed. We laid our heads on one pillow and looked directly into each other's eyes. We were searching, trying to find ourselves in each other, trying to blur the lines between us. We've been trying to blur them since the doctor first put Tish into my arms and I said, "Hi, angel." Since I first leaned over and tried to breathe her into my own lungs. Since I first put my mouth next to hers and tried to swallow her sweet warm breath and make it mine. Since my molars would ache when I played with her toes and I'd understand why some animals eat their young. Tish and I have been trying to collapse the gap her birth created between us since we turned from one body into two. But our separation keeps getting wider with each step, each word, each passing year. Slipping, slipping. *Hold my hand, honey. Come in. I'm scared, Mommy.*

I brushed a strand of her hair from her cheek and whispered, "I feel lonely in this skin, too. Remember when we were at the beach today, and we were watching that little girl wade into the waves and collect seawater in her little plastic buckets? Sometimes I feel like I'm one of those buckets of sea, next to other buckets of sea. Wishing we could pour into each other, mix together somehow, so we're not so separate. But we always have these buckets between us."

Tish has always understood metaphors best. (That thing you feel but can't see, baby, is like that thing you *can* see.) She listened as I told her about the buckets, and her gold-brown canyon eyes widened. She whispered back, "Yeah. It's like that."

I told her that maybe when we were born, we were poured from our source into these tiny body buckets. When we die, we'll be emptied back out and return to that big source and to each other. Maybe dying is just returning—back out from these tiny containers to where we belong. Maybe then all the achy separation we feel down here will disappear, because we'll be mixed together again. No difference between you and me. No more buckets, no more skin—all sea.

"But for now," I told her, "you are a bucket of sea. That's why you feel so big and so small."

She smiled. Fell asleep. I watched her for a bit and whispered a little prayer into her ear: *You are not the bucket, you are the sea. Stay fluid, baby.*

attendants

One morning, in the middle of the divorce, I called Liz to ask for parenting advice. Liz doesn't have children, so she is still sane enough to have perspective.

I said, "I know, I know, I *know* that all is well and everything is fine at the deepest level and all that shit. I know all of that. But I don't know it today. I'm worried that I ruined them. They're confused and afraid, and for Christ's sake this is the one thing I swore I'd never do to them."

She said, "Okay, Glennon, here is what I see happening: Your family is together on an airplane right now. You are the flight attendant, and the kids are passengers on their first flight. The plane just hit some serious turbulence, and the airplane is bouncing."

"Yes," I said. "That sounds about right."

"Okay. What do passengers do when turbulence hits? They look at the flight attendant. If the flight attendant appears to be panicked, the passengers panic. If the attendants are calm and steady, the passengers feel safe and follow suit.

"Glennon, you've been flying and living long enough to know that while turbulence feels scary, it won't take the plane down. Turbulence isn't deadly, and neither is divorce. We survive these things. The kids don't know this yet, so they are afraid. They are going to keep looking at your face for information. Your job right now is to smile at them, stay calm, and *keep serving the freaking peanuts*."

This is what I told myself every single day during the divorce, and a million times since: *Keep serving the freaking peanuts, Glennon.*

I was talking to a friend about this parenting mantra and she said, "Yes, turbulence doesn't take planes down. But planes do crash. What if the thing that's shaking your family's plane is *real*? What if your family actually *is* going down?"

A friend of a friend found out a year ago that her teenage daughter was dying of cancer. That's not turbulence. That's the crash we all fear. That's a family going down with the full knowledge that they won't all make it out alive.

This woman started drinking and drugging, and she didn't stop, so her daughter died while she was high. Her other two daughters watched their sister die without their mama present, because she had jumped ship. I think about this mother every day. I feel deep empathy for her. I also feel afraid for her. I fear that one day she will finally get still and that stillness will be so full of scalding regret that it will be impossible to stay.

We don't control the turbulence or tragedy that happens to our families. The plot of our lives is largely out of our control. We decide only the response of the main character. We decide whether we will be the one who jumps ship or the one who stays and leads.

Parenthood is serving the peanuts amid turbulence. Then

when real trouble hits—when life brings our family death, divorce, bankruptcy, illness—parenthood is looking at little faces and knowing that we are as afraid as they are. Parenthood is thinking: *This is too much. I cannot lead them. But I will do the thing I cannot do.*

So we sit down next to our babies. We turn their faces toward ours until they are looking away from the chaos and directly into our eyes. We take their hands in ours. We say to them, "Look at me. It's you and me. I am here. This is more real than anything out there. You and me. We will hold hands and breathe and love each other. Even if we are falling from the sky."

Family is: Whether we're falling or flying, we're going to take care of each other through the whole damn ride.

memos

Every generation of parents receives a memo when they leave the hospital with their baby.

My grandmothers' memo: Here is the baby. Take it home and let it grow. Let it speak when spoken to. Carry on with your lives.

My mother's memo: Here is your baby. Take her home and then get together each day with your friends who also have these things. Drink Tab before four o'clock and wine coolers after. Smoke cigarettes and play cards. Lock the kids out of the house and let them in only to eat and sleep.

Lucky bastards.

Our memo: Here is your baby. This is the moment you have been waiting for your entire life: when the hole in your heart is filled and you finally become complete. If, after I put this child in your arms, you sense anything other than utter fulfillment, seek counseling immediately. After you hang up with the counselor, call a tutor. Since we have been speaking for three minutes, your child is already behind. Have you registered her for Mandarin classes yet? I see. Poor child. Listen closely: *Parent* is no longer a noun—those days are done. *Parent* is now a verb, something you do ceaselessly. Think of the verb *parent* as synonymous with *protect, shield, hover, deflect, fix, plan,* and *obsess.* Parenting will require all of you; please parent with your mind, body, and soul. Parenting is your new religion, within which you will find salvation. This child is your savior. Convert or be damned. We will wait while you cancel all other life endeavors. Thank you.

Now the goal of parenting is: Never allow anything difficult to happen to your child.

To that end, she must win every competition she enters. (Here are your four hundred participation trophies, distribute accordingly.) She must feel that everyone likes and loves her and wants to be with her at all times. She must be constantly entertained and amused; every one of her days on Earth must be like Disneyland, but better. (If you go to actual Disneyland, get a fast pass because she should never be forced to wait. For anything, ever.) If other kids don't want to play with her, call those kids' parents, find out why, and insist they fix it. In public, walk in front of your child and shield her from any unhappy faces that might make her sad, and any happy faces that might make her feel left out. When she gets into trouble at school, call her teacher and explain loudly that your child does not make mistakes. Insist that the teacher apologize for her mistake. Do not ever, ever let a drop of rain fall upon your child's fragile head. Raise this human without ever allowing her to feel a single uncomfortable human emotion. Give her a life without allowing life to happen to her. In short: Your life is over, and your new existence is about ensuring that her life never begins. Godspeed.

We got a terrible memo.

Our terrible memo is why we feel exhausted, neurotic, and guilty.

Our terrible memo is also why our kids suck.

They do, they just suck.

Because people who do not suck are people who have failed, dusted themselves off, and tried again. People who do not suck are people who have been hurt, so they have empathy for others who are hurt. People who do not suck are those who have learned from their own mistakes by dealing with the consequences. People who do not suck are people who have learned how to win with humility and how to lose with dignity.

Our memo has led us to steal from our children the one thing that will allow them to become strong people: struggle.

Our terrible memo is also why we stay busy with the trivial while the world our children will inherit crumbles. We obsess over our children's snacks while they rehearse their own deaths in active-shooter drills at school. We agonize over their college prep while the earth melts around them. I cannot imagine that there has ever been a more overparented and underprotected generation.

New memo:

Here is your baby.

Love her at home, at the polls, in the streets.

Let everything happen to her.

Be near.

poems

When Chase was little, we'd find him at our kitchen table drawing maps of the world and making lists of every country on Earth and its capital. He'd pass entire afternoons writing his own song lyrics, and we'd collect little poems he'd left all over the house.

When he turned thirteen, we bought him a cell phone because he desperately wanted one and we wanted to make him happy. Slowly we watched him fade away. He stopped drawing maps and reading and writing, and we stopped finding poems around the house. When he was with us, I could sense his need to be *there* instead. So even when he wasn't on his phone, he was gone. He was just hovering among us. His eyes changed. They became a little duller and heavier. They'd been the brightest eyes I'd ever seen, and then, one day, they just weren't. In his phone, Chase had found a place easier to exist in than inside his own skin.

That was tragic, because inside the itchiness of our own skin is where we discover who we are. When we are bored, we ask ourselves: What do I want to do with myself? We are guided toward certain things: a pen and paper, a guitar, the forest in the backyard, a soccer ball, a spatula. The moment after we don't know what to do with ourselves is the moment we find ourselves. Right after itchy boredom is self-discovery. But we have to hang in there long enough without bailing.

There is so much about phones and children that parents worry about. We worry that we are raising children with commodified views of sex, lack of real connection, filtered concepts of what it means to be human. But I find myself worrying most that when we hand our children phones we steal their boredom from them. As a result, we are raising a generation of writers who will never start writing, artists who will never start doodling, chefs who will never make a mess of the kitchen, athletes who will never kick a ball against a wall, musicians who will never pick up their aunt's guitar and start strumming.

I was once talking to a Silicon Valley executive who had played an integral role in the creation and proliferation of cell phones. I asked how old her kids had been when she'd bought them phones. She laughed and said, "Oh, my kids don't have phones." "Ah," I said. *Don't get your kids high on your own supply.* Those who made the phones are creative people, and they want their children to become people who create, not just consume. They don't want their children searching for themselves out there; they want them discovering themselves in here. They know that phones were designed to keep us addicted to exterior life and that if we never dive inward, we never become who we were meant to be.

Abby and Craig and I talked about Chase's slow fade incessantly, but we didn't do anything about it. I knew in my gut that Chase was becoming addicted to his phone and that this was interrupting his growth and peace. But I was afraid that if I took the phone, he'd be left behind and left out. He'd be so different from the others. It took me two more years to re-member that fear of being different is a terrible reason for a parent to avoid doing what her child needs her to do.

When Chase was a freshman in high school, I asked him to take a walk with me. As we made our way down our driveway and to the sidewalk, I turned to my bright, beautiful boy and said, "I make a lot of mistakes parenting you. But I only know they are mistakes in retrospect. I've never made a decision for you that I know, in real time, is wrong for you. Until now. I know I'm not doing right by you—letting you keep that phone in your life. I know that if I took it away, you'd be more con-tent again. You'd be present. You might have less contact with all your peers, but you'd have more real connection with your friends. You'd probably start reading again, and you'd live in-side that beautiful brain and heart of yours instead of the cy-berworld. We'd waste less of our precious time together.

"I know this. I know what I need to do for you, and I'm not doing it. I think it's because all of your friends have phones and I don't want you to have to be different. The 'But everybody's doing it' reason. But then I think about how it's not all that unusual for everybody to be doing something that we later find out is addictive and deadly. Like smoking; everybody was doing that a couple decades ago."

Chase was quiet for a while. We kept walking. Then he said, "I read this thing that said that kids are getting more de-pressed and stressed than ever because of phones. It also said we can't talk to each other as well. I notice those things about my-self sometimes lately. I also read that Ed Sheeran gave up his phone."

"Why do you imagine he did that?"

"He said he wants to create things instead of looking at things other people create, and he wants to see the world through his own eyes instead of through a screen. I think I'd probably be happier without my phone. Sometimes I feel like I have to check it, like it controls me. It's like a job I don't want or get paid for or anything. It feels stressful sometimes."

"Okay," I said.

Chase and Tish both decided to quit social media and use their phones only for texting. We're going to wait until high school to get Amma a phone. We do not want to give her a job while she's so young. We want to give her the gift of boredom so she can discover who she is before she learns what the world wants her to be. We've decided that our job as her parents is not to keep her happy. Our job is to keep her human.

This is not a story about phones. This is a story about Knowing.

Brave parenting is listening to the Knowing—ours and our children's. It's doing what's true and beautiful for our child no matter how countercultural it seems. It's about how when we know what our children need, we don't pretend not to know.

boys

I have been raising my daughters to be feminists since they were in utero. I knew the world's training would begin the second they were born, and I wanted them to be ready. Ready meant having an internal narrative about what it means to be a woman that they could weigh against the world's narrative. I did not have an alternative narrative as a child, so when the world told me that a real girl is small, quiet, pretty, accommodating, and pleasant, I believed that this was the Truth. I breathed in those lies, and they made me very sick. Children are either taught by the adults in their lives to see cages and resist them, or they are trained by our culture to surrender to them. Girls born into a patriarchal society become either shrewd or sick. It's one or the other.

I wanted my girls to know this: You are a human being, and your birthright is to remain fully human. So you get to be everything: loud quiet bold smart careful impulsive creative joyful big angry curious ravenous ambitious. You are allowed to take up space on this earth with your feelings, your ideas, your body. You do not need to shrink. You do not need to hide any part of yourself, ever.

It's a lifelong battle for a woman to stay whole and free in a world hell-bent on caging her. I wanted to give my girls whatever they'd need to fight for their full humanity. Truth is the only weapon that can beat the pervasive lies the world will tell them.

So I'd place headphones over my watermelon belly at night and play audiobooks about brave, complicated women. After they were born, I'd rock my daughters to sleep with stories about women who had broken out of their cultures' cages to live free and offer their gifts to the world. As they grew, we'd go for walks and guess the careers of the women passing by: "I bet she's an engineer, a CEO, an Olympic athlete!" When another mother jokingly mentioned my daughter's bossiness, I'd say, "Isn't it great? She's a leader." When my girls lost a game and became furious, I'd say, "It's okay to be angry." When they started school and began to consider dimming and shrinking themselves, I'd say, "Keep raising your hand, honey. You can be your bold, brilliant self out there in the world. You can be sure of yourself and still be a girl."

It worked. As they grew, they'd come home from school and ask why the winner on the four-square court was always called "King." They'd ask their teachers why all the language in the constitution was *He*. They insisted that we transfer from their Christian elementary school because the teacher refused to entertain the idea of referring to God as She. When Tish's soccer jersey was issued to her with "Lady Bruins" on it, she led a revolt, demanding that either the "Lady" be removed from the girls' jerseys or "Gentleman" be added to the boys' jerseys. Amma wore suits to school, and when classmates called her a boy, she shrugged. When I complained about missing my appointment to dye my gray roots, Tish asked, "Why are you trying to change who you are?"

Five years ago, I was cleaning up the kitchen while CNN droned on. I walked over to flip the channel, but then I noticed a particular and disturbing pattern in the reporting.

The first story was about several white male government officials who had been caught lying and cheating to keep their power. The second story included footage of a police officer brutally beating an unarmed black teenager. Then these stories:

A fifteen-year-old school shooter who killed three classmates, one of whom was a girl who had rejected his advances.

Members of a lacrosse team had been charged with gang rape.

A college boy had been killed in a hazing incident.

A middle school gay boy had hung himself because of bullying at school.

A thirty-five-year-old decorated veteran had just "succumbed to PTSD."

I stared openmouthed at the TV and thought:

Oh my God.

This is what it looks like for boys to try to comply with our culture's directions.

They are not allowed to be whole, either.

Boys are in cages, too.

Boys who believe that real men are all-powerful will cheat and lie and steal to claim and keep power.

Boys who believe that girls exist to validate them will take a woman's rejection as a personal affront to their masculinity.

Boys who believe that open, vulnerable connection between men is shameful will violently hate gay boys.

Boys who believe that men don't cry will become men who rage.

Boys who learn that pain is weakness will die before they ask for help.

Being an American boy is a setup. We train boys to believe that the way to become a man is to objectify and conquer women, value wealth and power above all, and suppress any emotions other than competitiveness and rage. Then we are stunned when our boys become exactly what we have trained them to be. Our boys cannot follow our directions, but they are cheating and dying and killing as they try to. Everything that makes a boy human is a "real man's" dirty secret.

Our men are caged, too. The parts of themselves they must hide to fit into those cages are the slices of their humanity that our culture has labeled "feminine"—traits like mercy, tenderness, softness, quietness, kindness, humility, uncertainty, empathy, connection. We tell them, "Don't be these things, because these are feminine things to be. Be anything but feminine."

The problem is that the parts of themselves that our boys have been banished from are not feminine traits; they are human traits. There is no such thing as a feminine quality, because there is no such thing as masculinity or femininity. "Femininity" is just a set of human characteristics a culture pours into a bucket and slaps with the label "feminine."

Gender is not wild, it's prescribed. When we say, "Girls are nurturing and boys are ambitious. Girls are soft and boys are tough. Girls are emotional and boys are stoic," we are not telling truths, we are sharing beliefs—beliefs that have become mandates. If these statements seem true, it's because everyone has been so well programmed. Human qualities are not gendered. What *is* gendered is permission to express certain traits. Why? Why would our culture prescribe such strict gender roles? And why would it be so important for our culture to label all tenderness and mercy as *feminine*?

Because *disallowing the expression of these qualities is the way the status quo keeps its power.* In a culture as imbalanced as ours—in which a few hoard billions while others starve, in which wars are fought for oil, in which children are shot and killed while gun manufacturers and politicians collect the blood money—mercy, humanity, and vulnerability cannot be tolerated. Mercy and empathy are great threats to an unjust society.

So how does power squash the expression of these traits? In a misogynistic culture, all that is needed is to label them feminine. Then we can forever discount them in women and forever shame them out of men. Ta-da: no more messy, world-changing tenderness to deal with. We can continue on without our shared humanity challenging the status quo in any way.

I stood and stared at the TV. I thought back on how I had prepared my girls from day one to fight for their humanity. I thought:

Fuck.

I have a son, too.

I do not recall rocking my son to sleep with stories about tender men. I do not remember pointing to men passing by: "I bet he's a poet, a teacher, a devoted father." When an adult mentioned my son's sensitivity, I don't remember saying, "Isn't it great? His tenderness is his strength." When he started school, I do not recall saying, "You can be quiet, sad, merciful, small, vulnerable, loving, and kind out there in the world. You can be unsure of yourself and still be a boy." I do not remember saying to him, "Girls are not for conquering. They do not exist to play supporting roles in the stories of men. They exist all on their own."

I want my son to keep his humanity. I want him to stay whole. I do not want him to become sick; I want him to be shrewd. I do not want him to surrender to cages he must slowly die inside or kill his way out of. I do not want him to become another unconscious brick that power uses to build fortresses around itself. I want him to know the true story, which is that he is free to be fully human, forever.

M y son is an accomplished student-athlete. He takes tough classes, stays up all hours of the night studying, then wakes up early to go to practice. Until a few months ago, I used that as an excuse to let him slack off at home. I straightened his room for him while he was at school, I did his laundry, and I cleaned up the nightly mess he left out in the family room.

One evening, he asked to skip the dishes to go finish his homework. I let him go while Abby, the girls, and I finished up. That night in bed, Abby said, "Babe, I know it's out of love, but you cater to Chase, and he takes advantage of it."

I said, "That's ridiculous!" and then I lay in bed and stared at the ceiling for an hour.

The next day I turned on the TV and saw a commercial about a couple who had just become parents. The young mother left the baby with his father to return to work for the first time. The camera followed the father around the house as their Alexa chirped constant reminders that the mother had programmed the night before: "Don't forget music class at nine! Don't forget lunch at noon, the bottle's in the fridge! You're doing a great job!" Viewers were meant to swoon at the sweetness.

All I could think was: Did this father just arrive on Earth? Is he *new* here? Why does he need minute-by-minute coaching in order to care for his baby? What did preparation for this day look like for this baby's mother? In addition to getting ready to go back to work, this mama spent the previous night thinking through every minute of her *husband's* next day. She anticipated each of his and his baby's needs, and then she trained Alexa to hold the father's hand all day so he did not have to think at all. But this father appeared to be a grown man who loved his son. There was no earthly reason why he would not be every bit as capable of caring for his son as his wife was. They were *both* new parents. How had one of them become so helpless?

Oh, I thought. *OH.*

The next day I left Chase a list of chores to do. He didn't finish them. When I confronted him, he said, "I'm so sorry, Mom, I've got this big physics test tomorrow."

I said, "No, *I'm sorry,* Chase. I've been sending you the wrong message. I have accidentally taught you that achieving out there is more important than serving your family in here. I've taught you that home is where you spend your leftover energy, out there is where you give your best. I need to course-correct by giving you this bottom line: I don't give a rat's ass how much respect you earn for yourself out in the world if you are not showing respect to the people inside your home. If you don't get that right, nothing you do out there will matter much."

Our boys are born with great potential for nurturing, caring, loving, and serving. Let's stop training it out of them.

Years ago, my ex-husband went out to dinner with an old friend who had just had a baby. They stayed out for hours, and when Craig got home, I said, "Tell me everything! What's the baby's name?"

Craig said, "Hm. I don't know."

I said, "What? Okay. How's it going at home? Are they exhausted? Is the baby sleeping? How's Kim doing with it all?"

"I didn't ask."

"Okay. How's his mother? Is the cancer getting worse?"

"He didn't mention it."

"Wait. What did you *talk* about for two hours?"

"I don't know. Work. Soccer?"

I remember looking at Craig and thinking: *I wouldn't trade places with him for all the money in the world.* I would not have made it through early parenting without honest friends to talk through how hard it all was. It must be so lonely to be a man. It must be so difficult to carry by yourself all the things we were meant to help each other carry.

I don't want my son to be tamed into loneliness. So when I get stuck carpooling Chase and his friends all over God's green Earth, I turn down the radio and say:

What was your most embarrassing moment this week?

What's your favorite thing about Jeff? Juan? Chase?

Hey, guys: Who do you imagine is the loneliest kid in your class?

How do you feel during those active-shooter drills when you're hiding in the closet with your friends?

In the rearview mirror, I catch them rolling their eyes at each other. Then they start talking, and I marvel at how interesting their inner thoughts, feelings, and ideas are.

I remember once one of the boys said something particularly vulnerable and the other boys giggled uncomfortably. I said, "Hey. Just remember that when you laugh at something someone has said, it's not about the person who spoke. It's about you. He was brave enough to be honest; you be brave enough to handle it. Life is hard; friends need to be safe places for each other."

Our boys are just as human as our girls are. They need permission, opportunities, and safe places to share their humanity. Let's encourage real, vulnerable conversations among our sons and their friends. Let's ask about their feelings, relationships, hopes, and dreams so they don't become middle-aged men who feel permitted to discuss only sports, sex, news, and the weather. Let's help our boys become adults who don't have to carry life alone.

M y friend Jason told me that for the entirety of his childhood, he had cried only in the bathroom because his tears would bother his father and mother. "Man up," they'd say.

He told me that he and his wife, Natasha, were trying to raise their son differently. They want Tyler to be able to express all of his emotions safely, so Jason has been modeling vulnerability by expressing himself more openly in front of his son and his wife. After he told me that he said, "This might be in my head, but I feel like when I try to get vulnerable, Natasha gets uncomfortable. She says she wants me to be sensitive, but the two times I've cried in front of her or admitted that I was afraid, I've felt her pull back."

Natasha is my dear friend, so I asked her about that. When I told her what Jason had said, she looked surprised: "I can't believe he noticed that, but he's right. When he cries, I feel weird. I am embarrassed to say that what I feel is kind of like disgust. Last month he admitted that he was afraid about money. I told him we would get through it together, but, on the inside, I felt myself thinking: *Man up, dude.* MAN UP? I'm a feminist, for God's sake. It's terrible. It doesn't make any sense."

It's not terrible, and it makes perfect sense. Since women are equally poisoned by our culture's standards of manhood, we panic when men venture out of their cages. Our panic shames them right back in. So we must decide whether we want our partners, our brothers, our sons to be strong and alone or free and held.

Perhaps part of a woman's freeing herself is freeing her partner, her father, her brother, and her son. When our men and boys cry, let's not say to them with our words or energy, "Don't cry, honey." Let's get comfortable allowing our men to gently and consistently express the pain of being human, so that violent release isn't their go-to option. Let's embrace our strength so our men can take their turn being soft. Let us—men, women, and all those in between or beyond—reclaim our full humanity.

talks

When Tish was nine, she and I went to our favorite bookstore together. As we walked inside, Tish stopped and stared at a magazine rack—a wall of cover models, each blonder, thinner, and more vacant than the last. All ghosts and dolls. Tish stared.

As usual, I was tempted to distract her, hurry her along, put it all behind us. But these messages cannot be put behind us, because they are everywhere. Either we leave our kids alone to make sense of them, or we wade in with them.

I put my arm around Tish, and we quietly looked at the covers together for a moment.

ME: Interesting, isn't it? What story are they telling you about what it means to be a woman?

TISH: I guess that women are very skinny. And blond. And have white pale skin. And wear a lot of makeup and tall shoes and barely any clothes.

ME: What do you think about that story? Look around this store. Do the women in this store match the idea about women these magazines are selling?

Tish looked around. A gray-haired employee was straightening books near us. A Latina woman was flipping through a paperback on the memoir table. A very pregnant woman with blue punky hair was wrangling with a cookie-eating toddler.

TISH: No. Not at all.

We drove home, and Tish disappeared into her room. Fifteen minutes later, she opened her door and yelled down the stairs, "MOM! HOW DO YOU SPELL PETITION?"

I googled it. Hard word.

A little while later, she came downstairs to the kitchen holding a handmade poster. She cleared her throat and began to read:

HELP SAVE HUMANITY

Dear world, this is a petition to show that I, Tish Melton, strongly feel that magazines should not show beauty is most important on the outside. It is not. I think magazines should show girls who are strong, kind, brave, thoughtful, unique, and show women of all different types of hair and bodies. ALL women should be treated EQUALLY.

I liked her idea so much. It wasn't enough for women to have equality with men; they needed equality with each other.

I cannot rid my children's air of all the lies they'll be told about what it means to become a real woman or man. But I can teach them how to be critics of the culture instead of blind consumers of it. I can train my children to detect those lies and get angry instead of swallowing them and getting sick.

TWELVE-YEAR-OLD ME: That's the truth about women. I will match it.

TWELVE-YEAR-OLD TISH: That's a lie about women. I will challenge it.

TISH: Chase wants me to join the same club he joined in middle school. I don't want to.

ME: So don't.

TISH: But I don't want to disappoint him.

ME: Listen. Every time you're given a choice between disappointing someone else and disappointing yourself, your duty is to disappoint that someone else. Your job, throughout your entire life, is to disappoint as many people as it takes to avoid disappointing yourself.

TISH: Even you?

ME: Especially me.

EIGHT-YEAR-OLD TISH: Keri doesn't like me.

THIRTY-EIGHT-YEAR-OLD ME: Why not? What happened? What can we do to make it better?

TWELVE-YEAR-OLD TISH: Sara doesn't like me.

FORTY-TWO-YEAR-OLD ME: Okay. Just a fact, not a problem.

TWELVE-YEAR-OLD TISH: Totally.

woods

My friend Mimi told me that she was concerned because her middle school son was spending hours on his phone behind his locked bedroom door.

"Do you think he's watching porn?" I asked her.

"No!" Mimi said. "He can't be. He's so young!"

"I just read that the average age kids discover porn is eleven."

"Jesus." Mimi shook her head. "I just feel bad spying on him. I mean, it's his phone."

"Nah. You pay the bill. It's your phone, he's borrowing it."

"I'm afraid of what I'll find," Mimi said.

"I know. Me too, every time," I admitted. "But what if he's already found porn? What if he's lost in that world by now? Don't you want to go in and find him?"

"I just have no idea what I'd say."

"Listen, I know plenty of adults who find certain kinds of porn to be liberating, but the porn kids come across on the internet is misogynistic poison. We have to explain that to them so they don't learn that sex is about violence. I just think that saying anything at all—even if we say it awkward and stumbling and afraid while our kids roll their eyes—is better than saying nothing at all.

"What if you said:

"Sex is an exciting and wonderful thing about being human. It is natural to be curious about sex, and when we are curious about things, we turn to the internet for information.

"But here's the problem with using the internet to learn about sex: You cannot know who is doing the teaching. There are people who have taken sex and sucked all the life out of it to package it and sell it on the internet. What they're selling is not real sex. It lacks connection, respect, and vulnerability, which is what makes sex sexy.

"This kind of porn is sold by people who are like drug dealers. They sell a product that fills people with a rush that feels like joy for a short while but then becomes a killer of real joy. Over time people prefer the rush of drugs to the real joy of life. Many who start watching porn very young will get hooked on the rush. Eventually they will find it hard to enjoy real sex with real human beings.

"Trying to learn about sex from porn is like trying to learn about the mountains by sniffing one of those air fresheners they sell at the gas station. When you finally get to the real mountains and breathe in that pure, wild air—you might be confused. You might wish it smelled like that fake, manufactured air-freshener version.

"We don't want you to stay away from porn while you're young because sex is bad. We want you to stay away from porn because real sex—with humanity and vulnerability and love—is indescribably good. We don't want fake sex ruining real sex for you.

"What if you said something like that?" I asked Mimi. "Do

not leave that sweet boy alone in the woods because you are too afraid to go get him."

We don't have to have answers for our children; we just have to be brave enough to trek into the woods and ask tough questions with them.

We can do hard things.

cream cheeses

One afternoon I opened my inbox and saw an email with the subject line "Mom, You're Up!"

The email was meant to inform me that it was my turn to provide breakfast for my kid's school athletic team after their early-morning practice. Each morning, a parent delivers a full spread of bagels, cream cheese, juices, and bananas to school. She sets up the buffet while the children practice so that after they finish, they can dine.

The night before I was to deliver the goods, I received another email from the mother of one of the athletes. She had a concern she wanted to share with me. She was worried that the other parents had not been providing sufficient cream cheese choices for the children. For example, last Friday there had been only two options, and several of the children hadn't liked either one of them and had been forced to eat their bagels cream cheese–less. She had a solution: "There's a bagel store close to the school that makes five different flavors of cream cheese. Might you be able to provide all of them?"

All of them. *Five flavors of cream cheese*.

Five flavors of cream cheese is not how to make a child feel loved.

Five flavors of cream cheese is how to make a child an asshole.

And yet I am a cream cheese parent. All of my friends are cream cheese parents. Cream cheese parenting is the result of following our memo: Successful parenting is *giving your children the best of everything*. We are cream cheese parents because we haven't stopped to ask: Does having the best of everything make the best people?

What if we revised our memo? What if we decided that successful parenting includes working to make sure that all kids have enough, not just that the particular kids assigned to us have everything? What if we used our mothering love less like a laser, burning holes into the children assigned to us, and more like the sun, making sure all kids are warm?

bases

One morning I woke up and read a story unfolding at our southern border. Children as young as four months old were being stripped away from their asylum-seeking parents' arms, loaded into vans, and sent without explanation to detention centers. I searched the web for Americans' reaction to this, certain that all would be as heartbroken and outraged as I was. Some were. Others were hardened. Again and again, I read: "It's unfortunate, but they shouldn't have come here if they didn't want this to happen."

Privilege is being born on third base. Ignorant privilege is thinking you're there because you hit a triple. Malicious privilege is complaining that those starving outside the ballpark aren't waiting patiently enough.

Despair is physical for me. With each new heartbreaking image and heartless response, I felt hope drain from my body. Hope is energy. That morning, I ran out of both. I shut down my computer and climbed into bed at 3:00 P.M. Abby tucked me in, kissed my forehead. Out in the hallway, I heard my daughter ask, "Is Mommy okay?" Abby said, "She will be. She's feeling it all now. She has to feel it all so she can use it. Just wait. Let Mom sleep. When she gets up, something amazing will happen."

What if we let ourselves feel it all? What if we decided that it is strength—not weakness—to let other people's pain pierce us? What if we stopped our lives and the world for things that are worth stopping for? What if we raised our hands and asked, "Can we stay here for a minute? I'm not ready to run out to recess yet."

I slept for twelve hours and then woke up at 3:00 A.M. on fire. By the time Abby walked out of our bedroom, I'd set up a command center in the dining room. As soon as she saw my face, the piles of papers, and the easel covered with phone numbers and ideas, she understood. She looked at me and said, "Okay, babe. Let's do this. First, though: coffee."

As soon as the sun rose, we called the Together Rising team: my sister, Allison, and Liz. One was on vacation, one in the middle of a big project at work, one caring for a sick relative. They stopped their worlds and set up their own command centers in the beach rental, in the office, in the hospital room. We began the way we always begin our responses to large humanitarian crises: We contacted the people on the ground who understood the crisis firsthand and knew which organizations were responding with wisdom, efficiency, and integrity.

Together Rising exists to turn our collective heartbreak into effective action. We do this by serving as a bridge between two sets of warriors: the everyday warriors across the globe who—in their kitchens and cars and offices—refuse to go numb to crises in distant countries and their own communities; and the boots-on-the-ground warriors who devote their lives to world-healing, life-saving work. With a most frequent donation of just $25, Together Rising has ushered more than $20 million over that bridge from heartbreak to action.

At Together Rising, we are not the warriors—we find the warriors. This is crucial work because the most effective teams are often not the large well-known organizations people tend to give to. The fiercest groups we've worked with have been smaller, scrappy, women-led teams—those already trusted by the affected communities and nimble enough to respond in real time. Our job is to find them, ask what they need to continue their fight, and listen deeply. Then we introduce them to our heartbroken people. Our people give in order to get these warriors the help they need to carry on with their work.

So we wrote up the story of the administration's lawless cruelty at the border and the warriors working to end it. We posted it for our community, and other brave, compassionate artists helped share it widely. Within nine hours, we raised $1 million to reunify families. Within a few weeks, we raised $4.6 million. We spent the next year funding and working alongside other organizations to hold the government accountable and return those children to their parents' arms.

One morning, I posted a video of my sister escorting a six-year-old boy named Ariel back to his family after having been separated from them for ten months. Ariel's father had brought him to the southern border to lawfully seek asylum. When they arrived, American border patrol took Ariel from his father's arms. He begged authorities to just deport them both—all he wanted was his son back. The officials refused. They deported him and sent Ariel into government custody alone. This father had to return to his community—plagued by extreme poverty and gang violence—and tell his wife that he had lost their son. He and Ariel's mother were losing hope that they would ever see their son again when a team funded by Together Rising found them in Honduras. A month later, the Together Rising team stood on the U.S.-Mexico border for nine hours with Ariel's father, mother, and sister until the authorities agreed to follow the law, allow the family to present for asylum, and move to reclaim Ariel. One week after she crossed the border with his parents, my sister picked Ariel up in Washington, D.C., and drove him to the airport to reunite with his family. Ariel told her that he was afraid because he didn't remember what his mom and dad looked like. When my sister pulled out her phone and showed him a picture, he beamed with joy, recognition, and relief. Minutes later, Ariel sprinted into his parents' arms—ending ten months of excruciating separation. The video I posted of the airport reunion was haunting: both beautiful and utterly brutal. Reactions of gratitude and rage flooded in.

That afternoon, I stood in the hallway of my daughter's school. Another mother approached me and said, "Can we talk?" Her tone made my stomach drop. "Sure," I said. We stepped outside.

She began, "I've been following you for a long while, but I unfollowed you today."

I said, "Okay. Sounds like you made the right choice for you." I began to step away.

Nevertheless, she persisted: "With all due respect, I have to ask: Why don't you care about protecting America as much as you care about protecting illegals? We follow the law; so should they. You know, I read that many of these parents *know* their kids could be taken from them. They know it, and they come anyway. I'm sorry, but I look at my daughter and I just think: I cannot IMAGINE doing that. I cannot IMAGINE."

I looked at her and thought: *Really? You can't imagine risking it all—doing whatever it takes—to give your child a chance at safety, hope, and a future? Perhaps you're not as brave as these parents are.*

P eople use one of two tones when they say the words *I cannot imagine*.

The first tone is one of humility, awe, softness, gratitude. There is a quietness about it. A *There but for the grace of God go I* quality.

The second tone—the tone this woman used—is different. It is one of dismissal and judgment. There is a definitiveness about it. A *Well, I would never* quality. We invoke that tone like a spell, like a clove of garlic around our neck worn to distance ourselves from a particular horror in case it's contagious. We look for a reason, for someone to blame, so that we can reassure ourselves that this horror could never, will never happen to us. Our judgment is self-protection; it's a cage we put around ourselves. We hope it will keep danger out, but it only keeps tenderness and empathy from coming in.

What I realized, right there in the hallway, is that when people use the first tone, it is because they *already are* imagining. They are using their imagination as a bridge between their known experience and the unknown experience. They are imagining themselves into the other human being's shoes, and that is making them tender because they can somehow—through the magical leap of imagination—see and feel what the *other* might see and feel. That's when I realized that imagination is not just the catalyst of art, it's also the catalyst of compassion. Imagination is the shortest distance between two people, two cultures, two ideologies, two experiences.

There is a little boy in my daughter Amma's fifth-grade class named Tommy. Tommy never brings in his homework, so the kids never earn the class reward promised to them if they all comply. Tommy falls asleep in class repeatedly, and the teacher has to stop to wake him, which interrupts her lessons and makes her cranky. Amma is baffled by Tommy.

Amma walked in the door after school the other day, threw her book bag down on the floor, and said, "Again! He forgot his homework again! We are never going to earn our pizza party, never! Why can't he just do what he's supposed to do?"

Thankfully, I remembered the power of imagination.

ME: This is frustrating.

AMMA: I know!

ME: Babe, why do you imagine Tommy might not do his homework?

AMMA: Because he is irresponsible.

ME: Okay. Do you think that you're responsible?

AMMA: Yes. I am. I always do my homework and I never fall asleep in class. I would NEVER do that.

ME: Okay. How did you learn to always get your homework done?

AMMA: You taught me to do it right after school. And you remind me every day!

ME: Okay. Do you imagine that Tommy has parents at home who can sit down with him and make sure his homework is done like yours do?

AMMA: He must not.

ME: Also, baby, why do you imagine Tommy is so tired
during the day?

AMMA: He must stay up too late.

ME: How late do you imagine you'd stay up at night if
you didn't have us at home making you go to bed?

AMMA: I'd stay up all night!

ME: What do you imagine might happen to you during
the day?

AMMA: I'd probably fall asleep a lot.

ME: Yeah. Maybe you and Tommy aren't all that different after all. You're responsible, Amma. But you're
also really lucky.

Amma still gets annoyed at Tommy, but she has her imagination to keep her soft and open. She knows how to imagine
her way into his shoes. I'm not sure it matters if what she imag-
ines is true. I just know that the softening matters. She is learning how to use her imagination to bridge the gap between her
experience and the experience of another, and this skill will
serve her, her relationships, and the world. I think a kid who
practices imagining why a classmate keeps forgetting his homework might become an adult who can imagine why a father
might risk everything to cross a desert with nothing but his
child on his back.

islands

Dear Glennon,

My teenage daughter just called us from her boarding school and told us that she's gay. We are happy for her. We believe that love is love. My problem is this: My parents are staying at our home for Christmas. They are fundamentalists who I know will spend the holiday trying to shame and "convert" her. How do I handle this?

Respectfully,

M

Dear M,

When Abby and I fell in love, we kept it to ourselves for a while. Then, when we decided to build a life together, we began to share our relationship with others: our children, our parents, our friends, the world. People had big feelings about our news. Sometimes their responses would make me feel afraid, defensive, angry, too exposed.

One night, Abby, who knows I understand life best through metaphors, said this:

"Glennon, I want us to think of our love as an island. On our island is you, me, the kids—and real love. The kind of love novels are written about and people spend lifetimes trying to find. The holy grail. The most precious thing. *The* thing. *We have it.* It's still young and new, so we're going to protect it. Imagine that we've surrounded our island with a moat filled with alligators. We will not lower the drawbridge to let anyone's fear onto our island. On our island is only us and love. Leave anything else on the other side of the moat. Over there, it can't hurt us. We're here, happy on our island. Let them scream fear or hate, whatever. We can't even hear it. Too much music. *Only love in, babe.*"

Every time an internet troll, journalist, or fundamentalist minister shared self-righteous judgment, I'd smile and imagine his tomato-red face screaming on the other side of the moat, while Abby, the kids, and I kept dancing on our island. None of it could touch us. But things got more complicated when my best friend, my champion, my mother showed up on the other side of the moat, carrying fear in both her hands, asking us to lower the drawbridge.

My mother lives in Virginia and we live in Florida, but we talk every single day. We are intricately intertwined in each other's lives. Recently we were talking before bed, and she asked about my plans for the following morning. I mentioned that I had a haircut scheduled and I was thinking about getting bangs. We said good night. The next morning, my phone rang at 6:00.

"I'm sorry to call so early, sweetheart, but I've been up all night worrying. It's the bangs, honey. You don't do well with bangs. You cut them and then you regret them, and it becomes a whole thing. Your life is stressful enough already. I am just worried that bangs are the wrong decision for your family, sweetheart."

If my decision to get bangs had kept my mother up all night, you can imagine her reaction to my decision to divorce my husband and marry a woman. I could hear her fear in every question and in the long silences between her questions. *But what about the kids? What will their classmates say? The world can be cruel.* She was shaken, and that started to shake me. That day she told me not to get bangs? I didn't. My mother loves me very, very well, so I've always trusted her to know what was right for me.

It's not the cruel criticism from folks who hate us that scares us away from our Knowing; it's the quiet concern of those who love us. My mom's fear started to pull me away from my Knowing. I lost my peace. I became defensive and angry. I spent weeks on the phone with her, explaining myself, trying to convince her that I knew what I was doing and that it would all be okay. One night I was talking to my sister, working myself up, replaying to her my most recent conversation with my mom. My sister interrupted me and said, "Glennon, why are you so defensive? Defensiveness is for people who are afraid that what they have can be taken from them. You are a grown-ass woman. You can have what you want. No one can take this from you. Not even Mom. This is yours, Glennon. Abby is yours."

We hung up, and I thought: *My mother loves me. And she disagrees with me about what is best for me. I am going to have to decide who I trust more: my mother or myself.* For the first time in my life, I decided to trust myself—even though that meant moving in direct opposition to my parents. I decided to please myself instead of my parents. I decided to become responsible for my own life, my own joy, my own family. And I decided to do it with love.

That is when I became an adult.

That night I told Abby, "I'm not going to spend one more second explaining myself or justifying our relationship. Explaining is fear preparing its case, and we are not on trial. No one can take what we have. I can't convince my parents that we're okay by talking incessantly about how okay we are. I think the only way to convince anybody you are okay is just to go about being okay and let them witness it. I don't want to leave our island to be an evangelist for us anymore. It's too tiring, and every time I go and try to convince other people that we're fine, I'm not here, with you—*being fine*. So I'm adding a sign to our island. This one isn't facing outward at the world, it's pointing inward, toward us, as a reminder. It says: 'Only Love Out.'"

No Fear In. No Fear Out.

Only Love In. Only Love Out.

The next day, I stood underneath a tree at my son's cross-country meet, trying to find relief from the hundred-degree heat. I was on the phone with my mother, and she was asking to come visit her grandchildren. Her tone was controlled, anxious, shaky. She was still worrying and calling that love. She just couldn't trust my Knowing yet. But for the first time, I did. I trusted my Knowing.

Here is the part of the story in which a mother and a daughter become two mothers:

I say, "Mom. No. You can't come. You are still afraid and you can't bring that to us because our children—they're not afraid. We raised them to understand that love and truth—in any form—are to be honored and celebrated. They haven't learned the fear you carry, and I won't have it taught to them through your voice and in your eyes. Your fear that the world will reject our family is causing you to create the very rejection you fear exists. Our children are not carrying the fear that you are carrying—but if you bring it here, they will help you carry it, because they trust you. I do not want that unnecessary burden to be passed to them.

"Is this the easiest path for me, for Abby, for Craig, for your grandchildren? Of course not. But it's the truest one. We are making a true and beautiful family and home, and I hope with all of my heart that one day soon you will be able to come enjoy it. But we cannot be the ones to teach you that you can love and accept us. I have to tell you this hard thing, which is that your fear is not my or Abby's or the children's problem. My duty as their mother is to make sure it never becomes their problem. We don't have a problem, Mama. I want you to come to us as soon as you don't, either.

"This is our last conversation about your fear for us. I love you so much. Go figure it out, Mama. When you are ready to come to our island with nothing but wild acceptance and joy and celebration for our true, beautiful family, we'll lower the drawbridge for you. But not one second sooner."

My mother grew quiet for a very long time. Then she said, "I hear what you've said. I am going to go think about all of this. I love you."

We hung up the phone. I stepped out of the shade and walked back to my family.

M, listen to me.

You have a child on your island who is doing what few teenagers are able to do: She is living from her Touch Tree. Her tree is small, just a sapling on your island. Do not throw open the door and invite in a storm that will take her out before she's had time to grow roots.

Protect your island for her. She is not yet old enough to be the keeper of the drawbridge; that is still your duty. Do not lower your family's drawbridge to fear—not even if it's from people she loves. Especially not when that fear is presented in the name of God.

A woman becomes a responsible parent when she stops being an obedient daughter. When she finally understands that she is creating something different from what her parents created. When she begins to build her island not to their specifications but to hers. When she finally understands that it is not her duty to convince everyone on her island to accept and respect her and her children. It is her duty to allow onto her island only those who *already do* and who will walk across the drawbridge as the beloved, respectful *guests* they are.

Tonight, sit down with your cobuilder and decide with honor and intention what you will have on your island and what you will not. Not *who* your nonnegotiables are but *what* they are. Do not lower the drawbridge for anything other than what you have decided is permitted on your island, no matter who is carrying it.

Right now, you are being required to choose between remaining an obedient daughter and becoming a responsible mother.

Choose mother. Every damn time from here on out, choose mother.

Your parents had their turn to build their island.

Your turn.

boulders

Dear Glennon,

I just brought my baby girl home from the hospital. When I put her down on the floor in her carrier, I forgot how to breathe. I don't know how to do this. I am so afraid. My mother didn't love me well. At least once a day I think, Why couldn't she love me? Was there something wrong with her . . . or me? What if it was me? How will I ever know how to mother my daughter if I've never known mothering love?
H

Dear H,
This is what I know.

Parents love their children. I have met no exceptions.

Love is a river, and there are times when impediments stop the flow of love.

Mental illness, addiction, shame, narcissism, fear passed down by religious and cultural institutions—these are boulders that interrupt love's flow.

Sometimes there is a miracle, and the boulder is removed. Some families get to experience this Removal Miracle. Many don't. There is no rhyme or reason. No family earns it. Healing is not the reward for those who love the most or best.

When a parent becomes healthy again, her child begins to feel her love. When the boulder is removed, the water flows again. It's the way of the river, the way of a parent's love.

Your parent—your sister, your friend, the one who couldn't love you—her love was impeded. That love was there—swirling, festering, vicious in its desperation for release. It was there, it is there, all for you. That love exists. It just couldn't get past the boulder.

You can trust me about this because I have been an impeded river. The boulder of addiction blocked my love, and all my family felt from me was pain and absence. My dad used to ask, *Why, Glennon? Why do you lie to my face and treat us so terribly? Do you even love us?*

I did. I felt all the love swirling and festering and the pressure of it all felt like it would kill me. But they couldn't feel any of it. To them, it didn't exist.

Then I got my Removal, sobriety, which was both a spontaneous miracle and excruciatingly difficult work. Eventually my love was able to flow to my people again. Because I was always the river, not the boulder.

Desperate people often ask me, "How? How did you get sober? What did your family do?"

They tried everything, and none of it had anything to do with my recovery. All the love in the world cannot move a boulder, because the Removal is not between the impeded and the ones who love her. The Removal is strictly between the impeded one and her God.

I am so sorry, H.

You deserved to have the love of your mother delivered to

you. You deserved to be soaked through to the bone with her love every day and every night.

But now I need you to listen to me.

The miracle of grace is that you can give what you have never gotten.

You do not get your capacity for love from your parents. They are not your source. Your source is God. You are your own source. Your river is strong.

Soak that baby girl of yours to the bone day and night.

Flow unimpeded.

bloodbaths

During my *Love Warrior* book tour, thousands of readers showed up across the country, expecting me to do what I always did: tell the truth about my life. But for the first time in a decade, they didn't yet know the truth of my life. I had shared that Craig and I were divorcing, but I had not told them that I had fallen in love with Abby.

I had a choice to make: I could reveal my new relationship before I felt ready, or I could stand in front of my readers and hide the most important thing happening in my life. The first option felt terrifying and also the clear way, because of my One Thing. My One Thing is my sobriety. For me, sobriety is not just about stopping something; it's about beginning a particular way of life. This way of life requires living in integrity: ensuring that my inner self and outer self are integrated. Integrity means having only one self. Dividing into two selves—the shown self and the hidden self—that is brokenness, so I do whatever it takes to stay whole. I do not adjust myself to please the world. I am myself wherever I am, and I let the world adjust.

I will never promise to be this way or that way, I will only promise to show up, as I am, wherever I am. That's it, and that's all. People will like me or not, but being liked is not my One Thing; integrity is. So I must live and tell my truth. Folks will come around or quit coming around. Either way: lovely. Anything or anyone I could lose by telling the truth was never mine anyway. I'm willing to lose anything that requires me to hide any part of myself.

So I decided to tell the world that I was in love with Abby. The night before I made my announcement, one of my teammates said, "Here we go. Tomorrow is the bloodbath." I understood the trepidation. I knew that folks would be surprised and that they'd have a whole lot of questions and feelings.

Some would say with admiration, "I respect the hell out of you. What gave you the guts to do that?" Others would say with disdain, "I respected the hell out of you. What gave you the right to do that?"

I knew my answer would be the same, either way:

I left my husband to build a life with Abby for the same reason I left booze to become a mother eighteen years ago. Because suddenly I was able to imagine a truer, more beautiful existence for myself than the one I was living. And my way of life is to dare to imagine the truest, most beautiful life, family, and world—and to then conjure up the courage to make real what I have imagined.

In my thirties, I learned that there is a type of pain in life that I want to feel. It's the inevitable, excruciating, necessary pain of losing beautiful things: trust, dreams, health, animals, relationships, people. This kind of pain is the price of love, the cost of living a brave, openhearted life—and I'll pay it.

There is another kind of pain that comes not from losing beautiful things but from never even trying for them.

I've felt that kind of pain in my life. I recognize it on others' faces. I see the longing in the eyes of a woman who is next to her lover but feels totally alone. I see the rage in the eyes of a woman who is not happy but smiles anyway. I see the resignation in the eyes of a woman who is slowly dying for her children instead of living for them. And I hear it. I hear it in the bitterness of a woman who describes faking it so she can get up and finish folding the laundry. I hear it in the desperate tone of a woman who has something to say but has never said it. In the cynicism of a woman who has accepted the injustice she could help change if she were braver. It's the pain of a woman who has slowly abandoned herself.

I'm forty-four years old now, and I'll be damned if I'll choose that kind of pain ever again.

I left my husband and I am building a life with Abby because I'm a grown-ass woman now and I do what the fuck I want. I mean this with deep respect and love—and with the desire that you, too, will do what the fuck you want with your own singular precious life.

The truth is that it matters not at all what you think of my life—but it matters supremely what you think of your own. Judgment is just another cage we live in so we don't have to feel, know, and imagine. Judgment is self-abandonment. You are not here to waste your time deciding whether my life is true and beautiful enough for you. You are here to decide if your life, relationships, and world are true and beautiful enough for you. And if they are not and you dare to admit they are not, you must decide if you have the guts, the right—perhaps even the duty—to burn to the ground that which is not true and beautiful enough and get started building what is.

That is what I want to model now, because that is what I want for all of us. I want us all to grow so comfortable in our own feelings, our own Knowing, our own imagination that we become more committed to our own joy, freedom, and integrity than we are to manipulating what others think of us. I want us to refuse to betray ourselves. Because what the world needs right now in order to evolve is to watch one woman at a time live her truest, most beautiful life without asking for permission or offering explanation.

So the next morning, I woke up, poured myself some coffee, opened my computer, and took a long, deep breath. Then I posted—to a million people—a picture of Abby and me snuggling on our front-porch swing, her strumming a guitar, both of us looking directly into the camera. We looked certain. Content. Settled. Relieved. I wrote that Abby and I were in love and planned to build a life together, along with the kids and their father. I didn't write much more than that. I was careful not to apologize or explain or justify. I just let it stand. Then I walked away and reminded myself that I was responsible for telling the truth but not for anyone's reaction to it. I'd done my part.

My sister called me an hour later, and her voice was trembling. "Sissy," she said. "You won't believe what's happening. Please sit down and read what our people are saying. What they're doing. How this community is showing up for you and Abby."

I logged on and saw thousands of gorgeous, kind, gracious, intelligent, spacious, gentle, nuanced comments. They were from a community of people who understood that they did not have to understand me to love me. It was not a bloodbath. It was more of a baptism. They seemed to say, "Welcome to the world, Glennon. We've got you."

That night, a friend called and said, "Glennon, here's what I've been thinking about all day: You made this community for other women. But maybe it was actually for you. All this time you've been creating the net that one day you'd need to fall into."

May we all live in communities where every person's truest Self is both held and free.

racists

I was eleven years old when I started treatment for bulimia. Back then, the mental health world treated eating disorders differently than it does now. When a child got sick, it was assumed that she was broken. We didn't yet understand that many sick children are canaries in coal mines, passively inhaling toxins in the air of their families or cultures or both. So I was separated, sent away to therapists and doctors who tried to fix me instead of trying to fix the toxins I was breathing.

When I was in high school, a therapist finally asked my family to attend one of my sessions. After a few minutes, she turned to my dad and asked, "Can you imagine how you might be inadvertently contributing to Glennon's illness?" My dad became very angry. He stood up and walked out of the room. I understood why. My dad's first priority was to be a good father. He held so tightly to the identity of good father that he couldn't dare to imagine that he might in any way have hurt his little girl. In his mind, good fathers do not contribute to family dysfunction. They do, of course, all the time, because good fathers are still human. In retrospect, I can see that our family had ideas about food, control, and bodies that would have been healthy for all of us to excavate, pull out into the light, and clear up. But my dad's refusal to look inward meant that I was on my own for a long while. Nobody else was going to turn their insides out but me.

Decades after that day in the therapist's office, Donald Trump was elected president. A friend called me and said, "This is the apocalypse. This is the end of our country as we know it."

I said, "I hope so. Apocalypse means uncovering. Gotta uncover before you can recover."

She said, "Oh, God, not more recovery talk. Not now."

"No, listen—this feels to me like we've hit rock bottom! Maybe that means we're finally ready for the steps. Maybe we'll admit that our country has become unmanageable. Maybe we'll take a moral inventory and face our open family secret: that this nation—founded upon 'liberty and justice for all'— was built while murdering, enslaving, raping, and subjugating millions. Maybe we'll admit that liberty and justice for all has always meant liberty for white straight wealthy men. Then maybe we'll gather the entire family at the table—the women and the gay and black and brown folks and those in power—so that we can begin the long, hard work of making amends. I've seen this process heal people and families. Maybe our nation can heal this way, too."

I was adamant and righteous. But I'd forgotten that sick systems are made up of sick people. People like me. In order to get healthy, everybody has to stay in the room and turn themselves inside out. No family recovers until each member recovers.

was thinking about that conversation with my friend when I decided it was time to talk to my daughters. I sat on my family room couch and patted a spot to my left and one to my right. I said, "Come here, girls." They sat down and looked up at me. I told them that, a year before, a man who was white walked into a church and shot and killed nine people who were black.

Then I told my daughters for the first time about a black boy their brother's age, who was walking home and was chased down and murdered. I told them that the killer said he thought the boy had a gun, but what the boy really had was a bag of Skittles. Amma said, "Why did that man think Trayvon's candy was a gun?" I said, "I don't think he really did. I think he just needed an excuse to kill."

We sat with all of this for a while. They asked more questions. I did my best. Then I decided that we had talked about villains for long enough. We needed to talk about heroes.

I went to my office to find a particular book. I pulled it down from the shelf, came back to the couch, and sat between them again. I opened the book, and we read about Martin Luther King, Jr., Rosa Parks, John Lewis, Fannie Lou Hamer, Diane Nash, and Daisy Bates. We looked at pictures of civil rights marches, and we talked about why people march. "Someone once said that marching is praying with your feet," I told them.

Amma pointed to a white woman holding a sign, marching in a sea of black and brown people. Her eyes popped and she said, "Mama, look! Would we have been marching with them? Like her?"

I fixed my mouth to say, "Of course. Of course we would have, baby."

But before I could say it, Tish said, "No, Amma. We wouldn't have been marching with them back then. I mean, we're not marching now."

I stared at my girls as they looked up at me. I thought of my dad in that therapist's office all those years ago. It was as if my girls had turned to me and asked, "Mama, how do you imagine we might be inadvertently contributing to our country's sickness?"

A week later, I was reading Martin Luther King, Jr.'s, famous essay "Letter from Birmingham Jail," and I came across this:

> I must confess that over the last few years I have been gravely disappointed with the white moderate. I have almost reached the regrettable conclusion that the Negro's great stumbling block in his stride toward freedom is not the White Citizen's Counciler or the Ku Klux Klanner, but the white moderate, who is more devoted to "order" than to justice; who prefers a negative peace which is the absence of tension to a positive peace which is the presence of justice; who constantly says: "I agree with you in the goal you seek, but I cannot agree with your methods of direct action."

This was the first time I had encountered language that defined the kind of person I was in the world. I was a white person who imagined herself to be on the side of civil rights, because I was a good person who strongly believed in equality as the right idea. But the white woman Amma had pointed to in that photograph wasn't staying home and believing. She was showing up. When I looked at her face, she didn't look *nice* at all. She looked radical. Angry. Brave. Afraid. Tired. Passionate. Resolute. Regal. And a little bit scary.

I imagined myself to be the kind of white person who would have stood with Dr. King because I respect him *now*. Close to 90 percent of white Americans approve of Dr. King today. Yet while he was alive and demanding change, only about 30 percent approved of him—the same rate of white Americans who approve of Colin Kaepernick today.

So, if I want to know how I'd have felt about Dr. King back then, I can't ask myself how I feel about him now; instead I have to ask myself: How do I feel about Kaepernick now? If I want to know how I'd have felt about the Freedom Riders back then, I can't ask myself how I feel about them now; instead, I have to ask myself: How do I feel about Black Lives Matter now?

If I want to know how I'd have shown up in the last civil rights era, I have to ask myself: How am I showing up today, in this civil rights era?

I decided to read every book I could get my hands on about race in America. I filled my social media feeds with writers and activists of color. It became very clear very quickly how strongly my social media feeds shaped my worldview. With a feed filled with white voices, faces that looked like my own, and articles that reflected experiences like mine, it was easy to believe that, for the most part, things were fine. Once I committed myself to beginning each day by reading the perspectives of black and brown people, I learned that everything was, and always has been, quite far from fine. I learned about rampant police brutality, the preschool-to-prison pipeline, the subhuman conditions of immigrant detainment centers, the pillaging of native lands. I began to widen. I was unlearning the whitewashed version of American history I'd been indoctrinated into believing. I was discovering that I was not who I imagined myself to be. I was learning that my country was not what I had been taught it was.

This experience of learning and unlearning reminded me

of getting sober from addiction. When I started to really listen
and think more deeply about the experiences of people of
color and other marginalized people in our country, I felt like
I did when I first quit drinking: increasingly uncomfortable as
the truth agitated my comfortable numbness. I felt ashamed as
I began to learn all the ways my ignorance and silence had hurt
other people. I felt exhausted because there was so much more
to unlearn, so many amends to be made, and so much work to
do. Just like in my early days of sobriety from booze, in my
early days of waking up to white supremacy, I felt shaky,
jumpy, and agitated as I slowly surrendered the privilege of not
knowing. It was a painful unbecoming.

Eventually it became time to speak up. I started sharing the
voices I was reading, and speaking out against the racism of
America's past and the bigotry and strategic divisiveness of the
current administration. Every time I did this, people got pissed
off. I felt okay about this because I seemed to be pissing off the
right people.

Much later, I was asked to participate in an activist group
led by women of color. One of the black leaders tasked another
white woman and me with the job of planning an online webinar for other white women with the intention of calling them
into the work of racial justice. Our mission was twofold: Begin
educating other white women and solicit donations to fund
bail and respite for black activists putting themselves on the
line day after day.

The other white woman and I accepted the job. On our
planning calls for the webinar, we decided that she would focus
on the history of complicity of white women and I would focus
on my personal experience as a white woman waking up to her
place inside of white supremacy. I thought that if I explained to
white women that the confusion, shame, and fear they would
experience in their early days of racial sobriety were predictable

parts of the process of unbecoming, they would be more likely to remain in the anti-racism effort. Also, they'd be better equipped to confront their racism privately, instead of mistakenly believing that their feelings should be shared publicly. This felt important, because black leaders were telling me that the ignorance and emotionality of well-intentioned white women was a major stumbling block toward justice.

I knew what they meant. I'd seen it happen again and again. If white women don't learn that our experiences in early racial sobriety are predictable, we think our reactions are unique. So we enter race conversations far too early and we lead with our feelings and confusion and opinions. When we do this, we are centering ourselves, so we inevitably get put back where we belong, which is far from the center. This makes us even more agitated. We are used to people showing gratitude for our presence, so being unappreciated hurts our feelings. We double down. We say things like "At least I'm trying. No one is even grateful. All I do is get attacked." People become upset, because saying "I am being attacked" doesn't accurately describe what is happening. People are just telling us the truth for the first time. That truth feels like an attack because we have been protected by comfortable lies for so long.

We are dumbfounded. We feel like we are always saying the wrong things and that people are always getting upset about that. But I do not think people become upset just because we say the wrong things. I think people are upset—and we are defensive, hurt, and frustrated—because we have fallen into the trap of believing that becoming racially sober is about saying the right thing instead of *becoming* the right thing; that showing up is based in *performing* instead of *transforming*. The way we show up reveals that we haven't yet done the studying and listening required to *become* the right thing before trying to *say* the right thing.

We are mugs filled to the brim, and we keep getting bumped. If we are filled with coffee, coffee will spill out. If we are filled with tea, tea will spill out. Getting bumped is inevitable. If we want to change what spills out of us, we have to work to change what's inside of us.

"How do I enter the race conversation?" is the wrong question in the early days of racial sobriety. We are not talking about a conversation to enter publicly as much as a conversion to surrender to privately. Whether we are in it to perform or to transform becomes evident by the way we take up space. When a white woman who is unbecoming does show up publicly, she does so with humble respect, which is a way of being that is quiet, steady, and yielding. Not with hand-wringing shame, because self-flagellation is just another way to demand attention. She has feelings, but she interrogates them within instead of imposing them on others, because there is a deep understanding that how she feels is irrelevant when people are dying.

I planned to share all of this on the webinar. My hope was that it might prepare participants for the early stages of racial sobriety and that this preparation might serve the larger social justice efforts of our activist group. We sent the plans for our webinar out to the leaders of our group for feedback and approval. We made their suggested adjustments, then posted online about the seminar. Thousands registered. I went to bed.

The next morning, I woke up to a text from a friend that said: "G, Just checking on you. I'm watching what's going down online. Let me know that you're okay."

My heart sank as I opened up Instagram. There were hundreds—eventually thousands—of comments, many of them from people calling me a racist.

What I didn't know back then is that there are several valid and contradictory schools of thought about how white women should show up in the racial justice movement. One view: White women—when accountable to and led by women of color—should use our voices and platforms to call other white women into anti-racism work. Another view: White women should only use their voices to point to people of color already doing the work. Those who subscribed to the latter philosophy were furious with me about this webinar.

Why would you try to teach instead of pointing toward women of color who are already doing this work? Why would you take up space in this movement when so many women of color have been doing this work forever? You offering a free course is taking money out of black educators' pockets. Offering a "safe space" for white women to talk about race is wrong—white women don't need to be safe; they need to be educated. You are canceled. You are a racist. You are a racist, Glennon. You are nothing but a racist. Everywhere, the word racist.

I was stunned.

I am not new to criticism. I am a woman who announced her engagement to a woman during a countrywide Christian speaking tour. I have been publicly ridiculed by and excommunicated from entire religious denominations. I'm used to the "other side" hating me; I wear that kind of backlash as a badge of honor. But friendly fire was new and excruciating. I felt idiotic and remorseful. I also felt terribly jealous of every single person who had decided to sit this one out. I thought of the quote "It is better to be quiet and thought a fool than to open your mouth and prove it." I felt defensive, hurt, frustrated, and afraid. I could not think of a single thing I was more terrified of being called than a racist. This was rock bottom.

Luckily, I am a woman who has learned repeatedly that while rock bottom feels like the end—it's always the beginning of something. I knew that this was the moment I'd either relapse with a couple shots of self-pity and resignation, or I'd double down on my racial sobriety and carry on. I told myself: Breathe. Don't panic and flee. Sink. Feel it all. Be Still. Imagine. Let it burn.

Eventually, I started remembering.

Each night when I was growing up, my family would sit down on our basement couch and watch the evening news together. It was the time of the War on Drugs. I lived in the suburbs, but in the cities things were clearly terrible. The news insisted that crack was everywhere, and so were so-called crack babies and welfare queens. Night after night we watched young black bodies thrown to the ground, rounded up en masse, pushed into cop cars. After the nightly news, the show *Cops* aired. Along with millions of other American families, my family would sit and watch *Cops* together. Every night, I'd see mostly white cops arresting mostly poor black men. For entertainment. We would eat popcorn while we watched.

Thirty years later, after the Charleston massacre, my parents' rural Virginia town buzzed about how to respond to the racial issues agitating Americans' consciousness. A local church invited the community to come together and address it. My parents decided to attend.

They sat in a large room with about a hundred other white folks. A woman stood up to bring the meeting to order. She announced that she and a few other women had decided to respond by sending care packages to the predominantly black school across town. She suggested that they break up into groups and choose items to collect. The room exhaled in relief:

Yes! Outward action! Performance instead of transformation! Our insides are safe!

My father was confused and frustrated. He raised his hand. The woman called on him.

My dad stood and said, "I'm not here to make packages. I'm here to talk. I was raised in a racist southern town. I was taught a lot of things about black people that I've been carrying in my mind and my heart for decades. I'm starting to understand that not only are these lies, but they're deadly lies. I don't want to pass this poison down to my grandkids' generation. I want this stuff out of me, but I don't know how to get it out. I think I'm saying that I've got racism in me, and I want to unlearn it."

My father is a man who spent his entire career in schools championing kids who didn't look like me. He is a man who taught us every single day that racism is evil. But now my father understood that a person can be good and still be sick. He understood that there is such a thing in America as a highly functioning racist. He'd become humble enough to learn that we can be good, kind, justice-loving people in our hearts and minds—but if we live in America, we're poisoned by the racist air we breathe. He had dared to imagine that he played a role in our sick American family. He was ready to let burn his cherished identity of "good white person." He was ready to stay in the room and turn himself inside out.

I am a feminist, but I was raised in a sexist culture. I was raised in a world that tried to convince me through media, religious organizations, history books, and the beauty industry that female bodies are worth less than male bodies and that certain types of female bodies (thin, tall, young) are worth more than other types of female bodies.

The images of women's bodies for sale, the onslaught of emaciated women's bodies held up as the pinnacle of female achievement, and the pervasive message that women exist to please men is the air I breathed. I lived in a mine, and the toxin was misogyny. I got sick from it. Not because I'm a bad, sexist person, but because I was breathing misogynistic air.

I became bulimic, and it's taken me a lifetime to recover. Self-hatred is harder to unlearn than it is to learn. It is difficult for a woman to be healthy in a culture that is still so very sick. It is the ultimate victory for a woman to find a way to love herself and other women while existing in a world insisting that she has no right to. So I'm working hard at health and wholeness every day. I'm an advocate for women's equality because, at my roots, I know the truth. I know what my body is for. It's not for men's use. It's not for selling things. It's for loving and learning and resting and for fighting for justice. I know that every body on this earth has equal, unsurpassable worth.

And yet.

I still have the poison in me. I still have all the biases that were instilled in me for decades. I still struggle to love my body every single day. Fifty percent of all my daily thoughts are about my body. I still step on the scale to check my self-worth. Subconsciously, I would likely still judge a thinner, younger woman to be worth more than a heavy older woman. I know that often my knee-jerk reaction is not my wild, it's my taming. So I can correct that misguided first judgment, but it takes me a deliberate effort. We become the air we breathe.

When I was thirty-five, I noticed that the wrinkles on my forehead were deepening and I found myself driving to a doctor's office and paying hundreds of dollars to have Botox poison painfully injected into my forehead to make my face worth as much as the younger, smoother faces on TV. I quite literally knew better. But my subconscious did not know better. My subconscious had not yet caught up with my mind and my heart, because it was (is still) poisoned. It took a conscious decision to stop poisoning myself. To stop paying to have misogyny injected beneath my skin. I am a fierce, forever feminist. But I still have sexism and misogyny running through my veins. You can be one thing, and your subconscious can be another thing.

I talk to women all the time about how the misogyny pumped into the air by our culture affects us deeply. How it corrupts our ideas about ourselves and pits women against each other. How that programmed poison makes us sick and mean. How we all have to work hard to detox from it so that we don't keep hurting ourselves and other women. Women cry and nod and say, "Yes, yes, me, too. I've got misogyny in me, and I want it out." No one is terrified to admit she has internalized misogyny, because there is no morality attached to the admission. No one decides that being affected by misogyny makes her a bad person. When a woman says she wants to work to detox herself of misogyny, she is not labeled a misogynist. It is understood that there is a difference between a misogynist and a person affected by misogyny who is actively working to detox. They both have misogyny in them, programmed by the system, but the former is using it to wield power to hurt people and the latter is working to untangle herself from its power so she can stop hurting people.

But then when I bring up racism, the same women say, "But I'm not racist. I am not prejudiced. I was raised better than that."

We are not going to get the racism out of us until we start thinking about racism like we think about misogyny. Until we consider racism as not just a personal moral failing but as the air we've been breathing. How many images of black bodies being thrown to the ground have I ingested? How many photographs of jails filled with black bodies have I seen? How many racist jokes have I swallowed? We have been deluged by stories and images meant to convince us that black men are dangerous, black women are dispensable, and black bodies are worth less than white bodies. These messages are in the air and we've just been breathing. We must decide that admitting to being poisoned by racism is not a moral failing—but denying we have poison in us certainly is.

Revelation must come before revolution. Becoming sober—from booze, patriarchy, white supremacy—is a little bit like swallowing the blue pill and slowly watching the invisible, deliberate matrix we've been living inside of become visible. For me, the process of detoxing from booze included becoming aware of the matrix of consumer culture that brainwashed me into believing that my pain was to be numbed through consumption. Detoxing from my eating disorder meant seeing the web of patriarchy that trained me to believe that I was not allowed to be hungry or take up space on the earth. And detoxing from racism is requiring me to open my eyes to the elaborate web of white supremacy that exists to convince me that I am better than people of color.

In America, there are not two kinds of people, racists and nonracists. There are three kinds of people: those poisoned by racism and actively choosing to spread it; those poisoned by racism and actively trying to detox; and those poisoned by racism who deny its very existence inside them.

I've decided that the people who called me a racist were right.

And wrong.

I am the second type of person. I am a white woman who has come to the conclusion that the reason people call me a racist when I show up to speak about racism is that I am showing up as I am and I have racism in me. By what I say and don't say, by the way I say it, people can see my inner racism on the outside. What they are seeing and pointing out is the truth.

Every white person who shows up and tells the truth—because it's her duty as a member of our human family—is going to have her racism called out. She will have to accept that others will disagree with how she's showing up and that they will have every right to disagree. She will need to learn to withstand people's anger, knowing that much of it is real and true and necessary. She will need to accept that one of the privileges she's letting burn is her emotional comfort. She will need to remind herself that being called a racist is actually not the worst thing. The worst thing is privately hiding her racism to stay safe, liked, and comfortable while others suffer and die. There are worse things than being criticized—like being a coward.

I am afraid to put these thoughts inside a book that will not be in people's hands until a year from now. I know that I will later read this and see the racism in it that I cannot see right now. But I think of the words of Dr. Maya Angelou: "Do the best you can until you know better. Then when you know better, do better." Doing our best now is an active thing, and so is knowing better. We don't show up and then wait to magically know better. We show up and then, when we are corrected, we keep working. We listen hard so we can know better next time. We seek out teachers so we can know better next time. We let burn our ideas about how good and well-meaning we are so we can become better next time. Learning to know better is a commitment. We will only know better if we continue unbecoming.

So I will commit to showing up with deep humility and doing the best I can. I will keep getting it wrong, which is the closest I can come to getting it right. When I am corrected, I will stay open and keep learning. Not because I want to be the wokest woke who ever woked. But because people's children are dying of racism, and there is no such thing as other people's children. Hidden racism is destroying and ending lives. It's making police officers kill black men at three times the rate of white men. It's making lawmakers limit funding for clean water and poison children. It's making doctors allow black women to die during or after childbirth at three to four times the rate of white women. It's making school officials suspend and expel black students at three times the rate of white students. It's making judges incarcerate black drug users at nearly six times the rate of white drug users. And—because of my complicity in this system that dehumanizes others—it is dehumanizing me. The fact that the programmed poison of racism was pumped into us may not be our fault, but getting it out is sure as hell our responsibility.

So when the moment comes—whether it's about my family, my community, or my country—when the energy shifts to me and the question is asked of me: "How do you imagine you might be contributing to our sickness?" I want to stay in the room, I want to feel, to imagine, to listen, to work. I want to turn myself inside out to help clear our air.

questions

Recently I was holding a town hall–type event in the Mid-west. There were a thousand women in the audience, a smattering of men, a few gurgling babies. After we opened up the event for questions, I noticed a hand slowly rise in the back of the room. A runner hurried to the back, slid along the pew, and asked the owner of the hand to stand. A woman with short gray hair and a gentle, serious face with deep wrinkles slowly stood. She wore a sweatshirt with an American flag and the word GRAMMA puffy-painted onto it. Her hand shook a little as she held the mic. I loved her instantly. She said:

"Hi, Glennon. I've been following your work for ten years, and I came here to ask you a question that I'm afraid to ask anyone else. I feel . . . confused. My nephew is now my niece. I adore him . . . I'm sorry—her. My granddaughter took a boy to homecoming last year and a girl this year. And now . . . you're gay, too? I don't mean any offense, it's just: Why is everybody so gay all of a sudden?"

The room fell still and silent. The sea of heads that was

turned toward this woman slowly turned back toward me. Eyes were wide. I felt the room's collective stress. For her, for me, for all of us. (Oh, God, was that offensive? Was that wrong? Is Glennon pissed? But also why *is* everybody so gay all of a sudden?) They were worried that we'd just crashed and burned. I knew we'd finally taken off. Blessed are those brave enough to make things awkward, for they wake us up and move us forward.

I said, "Thank you for asking a question most are too afraid to admit they have. Unasked questions become prejudices. Your niece and granddaughter are lucky to have you. Will you tell me your name?"

"Joanne."

"Okay. I do know why everybody's so gay all of a sudden. It's those damn GMOs, Joanne."

A wave of relieved laughter washed over the entire church. Some ladies laughed so hard that tears rolled down their faces as we all had ourselves one giant, collective, organic baptism. When the laughter died down, I suggested that we all take a deep breath. It felt so good to laugh and then breathe together. Everything doesn't have to be terrifying, after all. This is just life, and we are just people trying to figure each other out. Trying to figure ourselves out. After our breath, I said something like this:

There are wild, mysterious forces inside and between human beings that we have never been able to understand. Forces like faith. Like love. Like sexuality. We are uncomfortable with our inability to comprehend or control these mysteries.

So we took wild faith—the mysterious undefinable ever-shifting flow between humans and the divine—and we packaged it into religions.

We took wild sexuality—the mysterious undefinable ever-shifting flow between human beings—and we packaged it into sexual identities.

It's like water in a glass.

Faith is water. Religion is a glass.

Sexuality is water. Sexual identity is a glass.

We created these glasses to try to contain uncontainable forces.

Then we said to people: Pick a glass—straight or gay.

(*By the way, choosing the gay glass will likely leave you unprotected by the law, ostracized by your community, and banished by God. Choose wisely.*)

So folks poured their wide, juicy selves into those narrow, arbitrary glasses because that was what was expected. Many lived lives of quiet desperation, slowly suffocating as they held their breath to fit inside.

Somewhere, sometime, someone—for whatever courageous, miraculous reason—finally acknowledged her dragon. She decided to trust what she felt, to know what she knew, and to dare to imagine an unseen order where she might be free. She refused to contain herself any longer. She decided to speak her insides on the outside and just Let It Burn. She raised her hand and said, "Those labels don't feel true to me. I don't want to squeeze myself inside either of those glasses. For me, that's not exactly it. I am not sure what it is, yet—but it's not that."

Someone else heard the first brave one speak and felt electric hope flowing through his veins. He thought: *Wait. What if I am not alone? What if I am not broken at all? What if the glasses system is broken?* He felt his hand rise and voice rise with a "Me too!" Then another person's hand slowly rose and then another and another until there was a sea of hands, some shaking, some in fists—a chain reaction of truth, hope, freedom.

I don't think that gayness is contagious. But I am certain that freedom is.

In the name of freedom, we added more glasses. We said, "Okay, I hear you. Those other glasses don't fit. So, here's a bisexual glass for you! And for you, how about a pansexual glass?" We kept adding labeled glasses for every letter of the LGBTQ until it felt like we'd eventually use up the whole alphabet. This was better. But not exactly right: Because some glasses still came with fewer rights and greater burdens. And some people, like me, still couldn't find a glass that fit.

My hunch is that folks have always been fifty shades of gay. I wonder if instead of adding more glasses, we should stop trying to contain people within them. Perhaps, eventually, we'll rid ourselves of the glass system altogether. Faith, sexuality, and gender are fluid. No glasses—all sea.

But letting old structures burn can feel uncomfortable and disorienting. Rumbling freedom is scary because at first it feels like chaos. Pronouns and bathrooms and girls taking girls to prom, oh my! But "progress" is just perpetually undoing our no-longer-true-enough systems in order to create new ones that more closely fit people *as they really are*. People aren't changing, after all. It's just that for the first time, there's enough freedom for people to *stop* changing who they are. Progress is the acknowledgment of what is and what has always been. Progress is always a returning.

Maybe we can stop trying so hard to understand the gorgeous mystery of sexuality. Instead, we can just listen to ourselves and each other with curiosity and love, and without fear. We can just let people be who they are and we can believe that the freer each person is, the better we all are. Maybe our understanding of sexuality can become as fluid as sexuality itself. We can remember that no matter how inconvenient it is for us to allow people to emerge from their glasses and flow, it's worth it. Our willingness to be confused, open, and kind will save lives.

Maybe courage is not just refusing to be afraid of ourselves but refusing to be afraid of others, too. Maybe we can stop trying to find common ground and let everybody be the sea. They already are, anyway. Let it be.

permission slips

A fundamentalist Christian organization recently announced that I was excommunicated from "the evangelical church." I learned of this with great amusement. I felt like Kramer from *Seinfeld* when his boss tries to fire him from a job he never really had. "You can't fire me," Kramer says, baffled and defiant. "I don't even really work here."

I was talking to a friend about this and she said, "It's so awful. Why can't they understand that you were *born this way*? You can't help it! How cruel to punish you for something you can't even change."

Hmmmmm, I thought. *That's not exactly it.*

Sometimes we say things that we believe are loving but actually reveal our conditioning.

Things you *can't* help are things you *would* help if you could.

If I could change my sexuality, I sure as hell wouldn't. Sweet Jesus: I love sharing my life with a woman. I love how relentlessly we yearn to understand each other and how neither of us quits until we do. I love how we already do understand each other so well, because we are two women trying to free ourselves from the same cages. I love how our life together is one eternal conversation that we put on pause only to sleep.

I love having sex with my wife. I love the touches that are suggestions, and I love the moment we lock eyes and decide. I love how well we understand each other's bodies, and I love the liquid velvet of her skin. I love the softness, intensity, patience, and generosity of the during, and I love the after—the time outside of time—when we lie in each other's arms in silence and smile at the ceiling in relief and gratitude. I love how one of us inevitably giggles and says: *Is this really our life?*

I have been in a mixed-gender marriage and in a same-gender marriage. The same-gender marriage feels so much more natural to me, because there is no constant effort to bridge the gap between two genders that have been trained by our culture to love and live so differently. My wife and I are on the same side of the bridge already. Being married to Abby is arriving home after a long, cold, exhausting journey. She is the crackling fireplace, the shag rug, the couch I sink into, the blanket wrapped around me, and the jazz playing in the background that makes me shiver inside my blanket.

What I want to say is: What if I wasn't born this way at all? What if I married Abby not just because I'm gay but because I'm *smart*? What if I *did* choose my sexuality and my marriage and they are simply the truest, wisest, most beautiful, most faithful, most divine decisions I've ever made in my entire life? What if I have come to see same-gender love as a really solid choice—just a *brilliant* idea? Something I would *highly recommend*?

And what if I demand freedom not because I was "born this way" and "can't help it" but because I can do whatever I choose to do with my love and my body from year to year, moment to moment—because I'm a grown woman who does not need any excuse to live however I want to live and love whomever I want to love?

What if I don't need your permission slip because I'm already free?

concessions

Recently, Abby, the kids, and I were lying on the couch to-gether watching one of our favorite family shows. During an intense scene, it became clear that the family's teenage daughter was about to tell her parents that she was queer. She and her parents stood around their kitchen island and she said, "I have to tell you something. I like girls."

In the pause that followed, the TV parents and all five of us on the couch collectively held our breath.

The mother took her daughter by the hand and said, "We love you . . ."

I whispered, "Don't say it don't say it don't say it."

". . . no matter what."

Damnit. She said it.

I knew this show was trying to be progressive, to prove that these parents embraced their daughter's gayness just as much as they'd embrace her straightness. I wondered, though, if this girl had just told her parents that she liked boys, would the mother have said, "We love you no matter what"? Of course not. Because "no matter what" is what we say when someone has disappointed us.

If my son got caught cheating on a test, I'd dole out a consequence and then assure him that I love him no matter what. If my daughter told me that she'd just robbed a bank, I'd hold her hand and tell her that I love her no matter what. The "no matter what" would imply that even though my child had done something that fell short of my expectations, my love is still strong enough to hold her.

When it comes to who my children are, I don't want to be an Expectations Parent. I don't want my kids striving to meet an arbitrary list of preconceived goals I have created for them. I want to be a Treasure Hunt Parent. I want to encourage my children to spend their lives digging, uncovering more and more about who they already are, and then sharing what they discover with those lucky enough to be trusted by them. When my child uncovers a gem inside and pulls it out for me to see, I want to widen my eyes and gasp and applaud. In other words: If my daughter told me she was gay, I would not love her in spite of it, I would love her because of it.

What if parenting became less about telling our children who they should be and more about asking them again and again forever who they already are? Then, when they tell us, we would celebrate instead of concede.

It's not: I love you no matter which of my expectations you meet or don't meet.

It's: My only expectation is that you become yourself. The more deeply I know you, the more beautiful you become to me.

If someone tells you who they are, consider how lucky you are to be graced with that gift.

Don't respond with an eviction notice, a permission slip, or a concession speech.

Un-God yourself.

Gasp in awe and applaud with gusto.

knots

for abby

Tonight you and I are in a minister's office, somewhere in Texas. We're chatting before I go out to speak to the waiting crowd. You don't like these steepled, echoing rooms. You come with me anyway. You sit in the front pew and listen to me talk about God and the hunches I have about her.

You think I'm wrong to believe there's a God. But it's what you love and need me for. You borrow my faith like we borrow our next-door neighbor's Wi-Fi.

This minister said something that made you feel safe. You looked down at your hands. You said, "I don't feel comfortable in churches. When I was little, I knew I was gay. I had to choose church, my mom, and God. Or myself. I chose myself."

"Damn right," the minister said. She cleared her throat. I smiled at her. But "Damn right" wasn't exactly it.

I turned to you. Touched your hand. I said, "Babe, wait. Yes. When you were little, your heart turned away from the church in order to protect itself. You remained whole instead of letting them dismember you. You held on to who you were born to be instead of contorting yourself into who they told you to be. You stayed true to yourself instead of abandoning yourself.

"When you shut down your heart to that church, *you did it to protect God in you.* You did it to keep your wild. You thought that decision made you bad. But that decision made you holy.

"Abby, what I'm trying to say is that when you were very little you did not choose yourself instead of God and church. *You chose yourself and God, instead of church.* When you chose yourself, you chose God. When you walked away from church, you took God with you. God is in you.

"And tonight—you, me, and God—we're just visiting church. We three came back for a visit, to offer the folks here hope by telling stories about brave people like you who fight their whole lives to stay as whole and free as God made them. When we're done tonight, you and I will go, and God will go with us."

I thought you'd looked at me every way possible. But now. The way you look at me, in this minister's office, is new. Eyes wide. Watery and red. The minister disappeared when you looked at me like that. Just you, me, and God there.

"Wow," you said.

L ike that time your "G" necklace got a knot in it.
  You stood there, by the bed, grumbling.
  Threatening to throw it away.
  I asked you for the chain. Held it in my hand,
  Almost invisible—delicate white gold, impossible.
  You left.
  I kept at it for a while.
  Impressing myself with my patience.
  And then—one tug in the right place—it all came undone.

You walked back into our room,
I held it up, proud.
"Wow," you said.
You bent down, and I clasped it back around you.
I kissed your cheek.

May we lay more elegant ideas around our children's necks.

decals

When I was a young mother, exhausted, isolated, and dripping with children, I got a postcard from a local church offering free babysitting during the service. My then husband and I attended the following Sunday and found coffee, breakfast, music, a nursery, inspiring speakers, and welcoming couples everywhere. This church had identified every challenge in a young family's life and fixed them all for an hour. It felt like heaven. At first.

Then one Sunday, the preacher started discussing the "sins" of homosexuality and abortion as if they were the pillars upon which this church was built. My insides caught fire. After the service, I contacted the preacher and set up a meeting. I asked him, "Why—if your church is based on the Jesus who spoke incessantly about orphans and widows, demilitarization, immigrants, the sick, the outcast, and the poor—are you choosing abortion and gayness to hang your hat upon?"

After many circular arguments, he looked at me, sighed, and smiled. He said, "You are a smart woman. What you say makes sense—in the ways of the world. But God's ways are not our ways. You must not lean on your own understanding. You seem to have a good heart; but the heart is fickle. Faith is about trusting."

Do not think. Do not feel. Do not know. Mistrust your own heart and mind, and trust us. That is faith.

He wanted me to believe that trusting *him* was trusting God. But he was not my connection to God. My heart and mind were my connections to God. If I shut those down, I'd be trusting the men who led this church *instead of trusting God*. I'd be relying on *their* understanding.

The thing that gets me thinking and questioning most deeply is a leader who warns me not to think or question. I won't passively outsource my faith and my children's faith to others. I am a mother, and I have responsibilities. To all children, not just my own.

When hate or division is being spread in our religious institutions, we have three choices:

1. Remain quiet, which means we agree.
2. Loudly challenge power, and work like hell to make change.
3. Take our families and leave.

But there is no more silently disagreeing while poison is being pumped from pulpits and seeping beneath our children's skin.

So many parents have come to me and said, "My kid just told me she's gay. We've been sitting in this church for a decade. How must she have felt hearing what our leaders thought of her and assuming her mother agreed? How do I undo what she heard there? How do I convince her that I never really agreed with any of it, and that she's perfect just the way she is?"

The God memos we get as kids are carved into our hearts. They are hard as hell to buff out.

Everybody owes it to herself, to her people, to the world, to examine what she's been taught to believe, especially if she's going to choose beliefs that condemn others. She has to ask herself questions like "Who benefits from me believing this?"

After that preacher told me to quit thinking, I began thinking harder. I did my research. Turns out, the memo he was trying to pass me—"A good Christian bases her faith on disapproving of gays and abortion"—started being issued only forty years ago. In the 1970s, a few rich, powerful, white, (outwardly) straight men got worried about losing their right to continue racially segregating their private Christian schools and maintaining their tax-exempt status. Those men began to feel their money and power being threatened by the civil rights movement. In order to regain control, they needed to identify an issue that would be emotional and galvanizing enough to unite and politically activate their evangelical followers for the first time.

They decided to focus on abortion. Before then—a full six years after the *Roe v. Wade* Supreme Court decision—the prevailing evangelical position was that life began with the baby's first breath, at birth. Most evangelical leaders had been indifferent to the Court's decision in *Roe,* and some were cited as supporting the ruling. Not anymore. They wrote a new memo using freshly feigned outrage and rhetoric calling for "a holy war . . . to lead the nation back to the moral stance that made America great." They sponsored a meeting of 15,000 pastors— called The Religious Roundtable—to train pastors on how to convince their congregations to vote for antichoice, antigay candidates. This is how they disseminated the memo down to evangelical ministers, who passed it down to pews across America. The memo read, *To be aligned with Jesus, to have family*

*values, to be moral, one must be against abortion and gay people and vote
for the candidate that is antiabortion and antigay.*

Presidential candidate Ronald Reagan—who, as governor
of California had signed into law one of the most liberal abortion laws in the country—began using the language from the
new memo. Evangelicals threw their weight behind him, and
voted in a bloc for the first time to elect President Reagan. The
Religious Right was born. The face of the movement was the
"pro-life and pro-family values" stance of millions, but the blood
running through the movement's veins was the racism and greed
of a few.

That is how white evangelicals became the most powerful
and influential voting bloc in the United States and the fuel of
the American white supremacy engine. That's how evangelical
leaders get away with the stunning hypocrisy of keeping their
money, racism, misogyny, classism, nationalism, weapons,
war, and corruption while purporting to lead in the name of
a man who dedicated his life to ending war, serving orphans
and widows, healing the sick, welcoming immigrants, valuing
women and children, and giving power and money away to the
poor. That is also why all a political candidate must do to earn
evangelical allegiance is claim to be antiabortion and antigay—
even if the candidate is a man who hates and abuses women,
who stockpiles money and rejects immigrants, who incites racism and bigotry, who lives in every way antithetical to Jesus's
teachings. Jesus, the cross, and the identity "pro-life" are just
shiny decals evangelical leaders slap on top of their own inter-
ests. They just keep pushing the memo: "Don't think, don't
feel, don't know. Just be against abortion and gays and keep on
voting. That's how to live like Jesus." All the devil has to do to
win is convince you he's God.

My evangelical friends insist to me that their opposition to
abortion and queerness was born in them. They are sincere and

convinced. But I wonder. We all believe our religious beliefs were written on our hearts and in the stars. We never stop to consider that most of the memos we live by were actually written by highly motivated men.

I don't know if I call myself a Christian anymore. That label suggests certainty, and I have none. It suggests the desire to convert others, and that's the last thing I want to do. It suggests exclusive belonging, and I'm not sure I belong anywhere anymore. Part of me wants to peel that label off, set it down, and try to meet each person soul to soul, without any layers between us.

But I find myself unable to let go fully, because to wash my hands of the Jesus story is to abandon something beautiful to money-hungry hijackers. It would be like surrendering the concept of beauty to the fashion industry or the magic of sexuality to internet porn dealers. I want beauty, I want sex, I want faith. I just don't want the hijackers' commodified, poisonous versions. Nor do I want to identify myself with hijackers.

So I will say this: I remain compelled by the Jesus story. Not as history meant to reveal what happened long ago, but as poetry meant to illuminate a revolutionary idea powerful enough to heal and free humanity now.

There was a time on Earth—like every other time on Earth— when humanity had turned against itself. A few hoarded unspeakable riches while children starved. People raped and robbed and enslaved one another and waged wars against one another for power and money.

There were a few (there are always a few) wise enough to see this order of things as unjust, untrue, and unbeautiful.

They saw that killing one another for money is absurd because what lies within each person is more valuable than gold. They saw that slavery and hierarchy are evil because no one is born more worthy of freedom and power than another. They saw that violence and greed destroy the powerful just as they destroy their victims: because to dishonor another's humanity is to bury one's own.

They saw that humanity's only hope for salvation was a truer, more beautiful order of things.

They asked themselves:

What kind of story might help people see beyond the lie they've been taught that some are worth less and others more?

What kind of story might return people to their wild—to what they knew of love before they were trained to fear one another?

What kind of story might inspire people to revolt against and live beyond the religiously dominated hierarchical machine that was killing them?

Here was their idea:

Let's rethink the stories we've been telling about God. Let's dare to imagine that God is less like the powerful men who run the world. Let's imagine God is actually like the person those rulers just killed. Let's imagine that God is a vulnerable baby, born to a poor single mother, among the group most despised by the religious and political elite. He was the least of these back then. They pointed to him. God is in him, they said.

Had these wise storytellers lived in modern America, they might point to a poor, black transgender woman or an asylum-seeking toddler alone in a detainment center and say: God is in this one.

This one—the one on the outermost ring of the rankings we've made up about who matters. This one—the one farthest from whom we have centered.

This one is made of our same flesh, blood, and spirit.

When we hurt her, we hurt our own kin.

This one is One of us.

This one is Us.

So let us protect her. Let us bring her gifts and kneel in front of her. Let us fight for her and her family to have every good thing we want for ourselves and our families. Let us love this one as we love ourselves.

The point of this story was never that This One is *more* God than the rest. The point is that if we can find good in those we've been trained to see as bad, if we can find worth in those we've been conditioned to see as worthless, if we can find ourselves in those we've been indoctrinated to see as other, then we become unable to hurt them. When we stop hurting them, we stop hurting ourselves. When we stop hurting ourselves, we begin to heal.

The Jesus idea is that justice casts the widest net possible so that every last one of us is inside. Then there are no others—there is only Us. Inside one net we are free from our cages of fear and hate and, instead, bound to one another. The revolutionary idea that every last one of us is both held and free: That is our salvation.

girl gods

"Glennon, you refer to God as "she"—why do you believe that God's a female?"

I don't. I think it's ridiculous to think of God as anything that could possibly be gendered. But as long as the expression of God as female is unimaginable to many while the expression of God as male feels perfectly acceptable—and as long as women continue to be undervalued and abused and controlled here on Earth—I'll keep using it.

conflicts

I received an email recently from an old acquaintance at that church I left.

It said, "Can I ask you something? I know that you and Abby love each other so much. It's really something. At the same time, I still believe that gayness is wrong. I want to be able to love you unconditionally—but I'd have to abandon my beliefs. What am I supposed to do with this . . . *God conflict*?"

I felt for her. She was saying "I want to be free to love you, but I'm caged by my beliefs."

I wrote this back:

First of all, thank you for knowing that you have a choice to make. Thank you for not landing on: *I love you, but* . . . We know that Love has no buts. If you want to change me, you do not love me. If you feel warm toward me but also believe I'm going to burn in hell, you do not love me. If you wish me well but vote against my family being protected by the law, you do not love me. Thank you for understanding that to love me as yourself means to want for me and for my family every good thing you want for yourself and your family. Anything less than that is less than love. So, yes. I agree that you have a choice to make. You have to choose between loving me and keeping your beliefs. Thank you for being intellectually honest about that.

Second: I understand this conflict because I've experienced it. I still do. For a while I felt scared because I thought the God conflict was me challenging God. Now I know that it was God in me, challenging religion. It was my true self awakening and saying: *Wait. This thing I have been taught to believe about God, about myself, about others—it doesn't fit with what I know from my roots about love. What do I do? Do I reject what I know from my roots or what I was taught to believe?*

I can only tell you what I have come to know for myself.

Returning to ourselves is confusing at first. It's not as simple as listening for the voices inside of us. Because sometimes the voices inside of us, which we've assumed speak Truth, are just the voices of human beings who told us what to believe. Often the internal voice telling us who God is and what God approves of is not God; it's our indoctrination. It's an echo of the voice of a teacher, a parent, a preacher—someone who has claimed to represent God to us. Many of those people have been well meaning, and others have only sought to control us. Either way, not a single one of them has been God's appointed spokesperson. Not a single one of them has more God in her than you do. There is no church that owns God. There is no religion that owns God. There are no gatekeepers. None of this is that easy. There is no outsourcing your faith. There is just you and God.

Some of the hardest and most important work of our lives is learning to separate the voices of teachers from wisdom, propaganda from truth, fear from love and in this case: the voices of God's self-appointed representatives from the voice of God Herself.

When choosing between something you Know and something other people taught you to believe, choose what you Know. As Whitman said, "Re-examine all you have been told in school or church or in any book, and dismiss whatever insults your own soul."

Having the courage to dismiss what insults your soul is a matter of life or death. If those who claim to speak for God or Truth can convince you to *believe instead of Know,* to live from their rules instead of your roots, to trust the voices of middlemen instead of the still, small voice inside you—then they control you. If they can get you to mistrust yourself—to stop feeling, deny knowing, quit imagining—and instead rely only on them, then they can get you to *act* against your own soul. If that happens, they can get you to follow them, vote with them, condemn for them, even kill for them—all in the name of this God who is constantly whispering to you: *That is not exactly it*.

Perhaps the God conflict is not just about God. Perhaps it *is* God. Listen deep.

streams

Good art originates not from the desire to show off but from the desire to show yourself. Good art always comes from our desperate desire to breathe, to be seen, to be loved. In everyday life, we are used to seeing only the shiny outer layer of folks. Art makes us less lonely because it always comes from the desperate center of the artist—and each of our centers is desperate. That's why good art is such a relief.

People often tell me that my writing feels like a relief. What they feel next is a desire to respond to my offering by telling me their story. For many years I'd stay for hours after my speaking events while one woman after another touched my arm, saying, "I just need to tell you this . . ."

Eventually I opened a post office box and promised people that if they wrote down their stories, I'd read them all. Each week, letters pour in. Boxes of letters are piled up in my bedroom and office. I imagine I'll be reading them until I'm ninety. A few times a week I put down my phone and turn off the news, snuggle up in bed, and read letters. It is always such a relief. *Ah, yes.* This is what people are like. We are all so fucked up and so magical. Life is so brutal and beautiful. Life is *brutiful.* For all of us. I remember now. If you want to get jaded and numb, watch the news. If you want to stay human, read letters. When trying to understand humanity, seek out firsthand accounts.

One night, surrounded by letters that my sister and I had been reading for hours, we looked at the pile and thought: Many of these people have more than enough. Many don't have enough. All of these people are hungry for purpose and connection. Let's be the bridge between them. We decided to start Together Rising. That's how I became what they call a philanthropist.

Since Together Rising was founded eight years ago, our five-woman board and fierce volunteers have spent day and night frantically and relentlessly connecting suffering people with every resource within our grasp: money, service, sister-hood, hope. Since we connect with every person we serve, we've learned firsthand that folks are generally doing the best they can. Yet so many still can't put food on the table or get medical care for their sick mothers or keep the heat on or se-cure a safe space to raise their children. Every night we'd go to bed wondering: Why? Why are all of these people who are trying so hard—still hurting so badly?

And then one day, I read this:

> There comes a point where we need to stop just pulling people out of the river. We need to go upstream and find out why they're falling in.
>
> —*Archbishop Desmond Tutu*

When I started looking upstream, I learned that where there is great suffering, there is often great profit. Now when I encounter someone who is struggling to stay afloat, I know to first ask, "How can I help you right now?" Then, when she is safe and dry, to ask, "What institution or person is benefiting from your suffering?"

Every philanthropist, if she is paying attention, eventually becomes an activist. If we do not, we risk becoming codependent with power—saving the system's victims while the system collects the profits, then pats us on the head for our service. We become injustice's foot soldiers.

In order to avoid being complicit with those upstream, we must become the people of And/Both. We must commit to pulling our brothers and sisters out of the river and also commit to going upstream to identify, confront, and hold accountable those who are pushing them in.

We help parents bury their babies who were victims of gun violence. And we go upstream to fight the gun manufacturers and politicians who profit from their children's deaths.

We step into the gap to sustain moms who are raising families with imprisoned dads. And we go upstream to dismantle the injustice of mass incarceration.

We fund recovery programs for those suffering from opioid addiction. And we go upstream to rail against the system that enables Big Pharma and corrupt doctors to get richer every time another kid gets hooked.

We provide shelter and mentoring for LGBTQ homeless kids. And we go upstream to renounce the religious-based bigotry, family rejection, and homophobic policies that make LGBTQ kids more than twice as likely as their straight or cisgender peers to experience homelessness.

We help struggling veterans get the PTSD treatment they need and deserve, and we go upstream to confront the military-industrial complex, which is so zealous to send our soldiers to war and so willing to abandon them when they return.

If we are to create a truer, more beautiful world, we must be the people of And/Both. Let's keep pulling folks out of the river forever. And every single day, let's look upstream and give living hell to the ones pushing them in.

lies

My friend and I are lying on the couch, marveling, crying, and laughing about all we've let burn and rebuilt during the past couple years of our lives. When I say, "Then I left my family," she stops laughing.

She says, "Don't say that. Don't say things about yourself that aren't true. You didn't leave your family. Not for a single moment. You didn't even leave your husband, for God's sake. You left your marriage. That's it. That's what you left. And that's what you had to leave to *create* your true family. Please don't ever let me hear you say 'I left my family' again. Be careful with the stories you tell about yourself."

deliveries

I am a sensitive, introverted woman, which means that I love humanity but actual human beings are tricky for me. I love people but not *in person*. For example, I would die for you but not, like . . . meet you for coffee. I became a writer so I could stay at home alone in my pajamas, reading and writing about the importance of human connection and community. It is an almost perfect existence. Except that every so often, while I'm thinking my thoughts, writing my words, living in my favorite spot—which is deep inside my own head—something stunning happens: A sirenlike noise tears through my home. I freeze.

It takes me a solid minute to understand: The siren is the doorbell. A *person* is ringing my doorbell. I run out of my office to find my children also stunned, frozen, and waiting for direction about how to respond to this imminent home invasion. We stare at each other, count bodies, and collectively cycle through the five stages of doorbell grief:

1. Denial: This cannot be happening. ALL OF THE PEO-
   PLE ALLOWED TO BE IN THIS HOUSE ARE AL-
   READY IN THIS HOUSE. Maybe it was the TV. IS
   THE TV ON?
2. Anger: WHO *DOES* THIS? WHAT KIND OF
   BOUNDARYLESS AGGRESSOR RINGS SOME-
   ONE'S DOORBELL IN BROAD DAYLIGHT?
3. Bargaining: Don't move, don't breathe—maybe they'll
   go away.
4. Depression: Why? Why us? Why anyone? Why is life so
   hard?
5. Acceptance: Damnit to hell. You—the little one—we
   volunteer you. Put on some pants, act normal, and answer the door.

It's dramatic, but the door always gets answered. If the kids
aren't home, I'll even answer it myself. Is this because I remember that adulting requires door answering? Of course not. I answer the door because of the sliver of hope in my heart that if I
open the door, there might be a package waiting for me. A
package!

When I got sober, I learned that hard feelings are doorbells
that interrupt me, send me into a panic, and then leave me with
an exciting package. Sobriety is a decision to stop numbing and
blaming away hard feelings and to start answering the door. So
when I quit drinking, I began allowing my feelings to disturb
me. This was scary, because I had always assumed that my feelings were so big and powerful that they would stay forever and
eventually kill me. But my hard feelings did not stay forever,
and they did not kill me. Instead, they came and went, and afterward I was left with something I didn't have before. That
something was *self-knowledge*.

Hard feelings rang my bell and then left me with a package

filled with brand-spanking-new information about myself. This new information was always *exactly* what I needed to know about myself to take the next step in my life with confidence and creativity. It turned out that what I needed most was inside the one place I'd been running from my entire life: pain. Everything I needed to know *next* was inside the discomfort of *now*.

As I practiced allowing my hard feelings to come and stay as long as they needed to, I got to know myself. The reward for enduring hard feelings was finding my potential, my purpose, and my people. I am so grateful. I can't imagine a greater tragedy than remaining forever unknown to myself. That would be the ultimate self-abandonment. So I have become unafraid of my own feelings. Now when hard feelings ring the bell, I put on my big-girl pants and answer the door.

anger

For years after I found out about my ex-husband's infidelity, I was deeply angry.

He did everything that could be asked of a person who has hurt someone. He apologized profusely, began therapy, and was unwaveringly patient. I did all the right things, too. I went to therapy, prayed, committed myself to trying to forgive. Sometimes when I watched him with the children, my anger would fade and I'd feel relieved and hopeful for our future. But every time I tried to make myself physically or emotionally vulnerable to him, rage would flood my body. I'd lash out at him and then shut down and retreat back into myself. This pattern was exhausting and depressing for both of us, but I didn't know what to do other than wait for forgiveness to eventually be bestowed upon me by the heavens as a reward for my steadfast suffering. I assumed that forgiveness was a matter of time.

One evening, Craig and I were sitting on opposite sides of our family room couch. He was happily watching TV while I silently fumed at him. Somehow I was able to lift my perspective and look down at both of us. There I was, fired up with fury, and there Craig was, undisturbed and utterly unaware that I was miserable. All the fire was *in me*. None in him. I thought: *How can this anger be about him? He can't even feel it*. Suddenly I felt possessive and protective of my own anger. I thought: *This is happening inside my body. If this anger is in me, I am going to assume it is* for *me*. I decided to stop being ashamed and afraid of my anger, to stop being ashamed and afraid of myself.

From that moment on, whenever anger arose, I practiced staying open and curious. I sat with it. I let it be. My anger and I hung out and listened to each other. I asked my anger questions like "What are you trying to tell me? Not about him, but about me?" I started paying close attention to patterns in my body, because my body often clarifies for me what my mind is too convoluted and hopeful to accept. Bodies won't lie, even when we beg them to. I noticed that anger flooded my body whenever I opened myself up to Craig emotionally or physically. My anger lifted completely when I watched him with the children. Before I started paying close attention, I thought this meant that I was flip-flopping. But over time I began to understand that my anger wasn't arbitrary, it was incredibly specific. My anger was repeating, "Glennon: For you, familial intimacy with Craig is safe. Physical and emotional intimacy are not."

I knew this. My body knew this. And I had been ignoring what I knew. That is why I was so angry: *I was angry at myself*. Craig was the one who had strayed, yes, but I was the one who decided, day after day, to stay married, vulnerable, and angry. I was ignoring what I knew, and I was punishing him for forcing me to know it. There was nothing he could do to change what I knew. Maybe the question was no longer "How could he have done this to me?" but "How can I keep doing this to myself?" Maybe instead of forever repeating, "How could he have abandoned me?" I needed to ask, "Why do I keep abandoning myself?"

Eventually I decided to stop abandoning myself—which meant honoring my anger. I didn't need to prove to anyone else whether leaving was right or wrong. I didn't need to justify my anger anymore. What I needed to do was forgive the father of my children. I was able to do that as soon as I divorced him.

After the divorce mediation, Craig and I stood side by side in an elevator, watching the floor numbers light up one at a time while we descended. I looked over at Craig, and for the first time in years, I felt true empathy, tenderness, and warmth toward him. Once again, I could see him as a good man with whom I'd like to be friends. I felt real forgiveness. That was because for the first time in years, I felt safe. I'd restored my own boundaries. I'd begun to trust myself, because I'd become a woman who refuses to abandon herself to keep false peace.

I have friends who did find safety and lasting forgiveness inside their marriages after infidelity. What comes after betrayal cannot be striving, contorting, or suffering to honor an arbitrary idea of right or wrong. What comes next must be an honoring of self. We must disregard the *should* out there and face what is real in here. If constant anger is what is real in here, we must address it—both for ourselves and for the other. Because it is not kind to keep those we can't forgive close to us and punish them forever. If we cannot forgive and move on, perhaps we need to move on first, and forgiveness will follow. Forgiveness does not mean access. We can give the other person the gift of forgiveness and ourselves the gift of safety and freedom at the very same time. When both people become unafraid and unpunished, that is a good good-bye. Relief from anger is not something that is bestowed upon us; it often must be forged by us.

Anger delivers important information about where one of our boundaries has been crossed. When we answer the door and accept that delivery, we begin to know ourselves better. When we restore the boundary that was violated, we honor ourselves. When we know ourselves and honor ourselves, we live with integrity, peace, and power—understanding that we are the kind of woman who will be wise and brave enough to care for herself. Good stuff.

And there's more. Even *better* stuff comes when we go deeper. When we say, "Okay. I understand that this is my boundary." But what *is* a boundary anyway?

A boundary is the edge of one of our root beliefs about ourselves and the world.

We are like computers, and our beliefs are the software with which we're programmed. Often our beliefs are programmed into us without our knowledge by our culture, community, religion, and family. Even though we don't choose those subconscious programs, they run our lives. They control our decisions, perspectives, feelings, and interactions, so they determine our destiny. What we believe, we become. There is nothing more important than unearthing what we really believe to be true about ourselves and our world—and nothing unearths what we really believe faster than examining what pisses us off.

My anger at my ex-husband was a relentless doorbell trying to alert me that a major boundary of mine had been crossed. My boundary was the edge of this root belief of mine: *The most important values in a marriage are honesty, loyalty, and faithfulness, and when those are gone, I am no longer safe.*

That belief of mine was neither right nor wrong. Beliefs have nothing to do with objective universal morality and everything to do with each person's specific, personal one. In this case, I decided to accept and keep this root belief about marriage and loyalty because it served me, made me feel safe, and felt true to me. I accepted that delivery and brought it right into my second marriage.

But sometimes my anger delivers to my door a root belief that I don't want to keep.

Abby works hard and rests hard. Often in the middle of a weekday, she will lie down on our couch and watch zombie shows. When she does this, I get clenched and tight. I get agitated, then angry, because she is *relaxing at me*. I start tidying loudly and aggressively in the couch's vicinity. She hears my violent tidying and asks, "What's wrong?" I say, "Nothing" with a tone that suggests "Something." This dance plays out again and again: Abby relaxing on the couch and me getting angry about it and Abby getting angry that I'm getting angry.

We talk this out, again and again. You have not *seen* talking until you've seen the incessant talking of two married women who are introspective spiritual seekers and also sober so they have nothing else to do. We adore each other. We never want to hurt each other. We want to understand each other and ourselves, so we really want to get to the bottom of things. So we talk, and we talk, and we always seem to arrive at this conclusion: Abby is a grown woman, and she is the boss of herself. Glennon should stop feeling angry about Abby's decisions.

I always agree with this conclusion. My *mind* does, at least. But how do I get this memo to my body? What do I do with *should*? *Should* never helps me because I am dealing with what *is*. Layering a judgment on top of a feeling doesn't change the feeling. How do I not become angry? How do I not become . . . activated?

One day I walked into our family room and saw Abby jump

off the couch and begin straightening pillows, trying to look busy and productive for my sake. I stopped in my tracks and stared at her while a memory from childhood floated into my mind. When I was young, if I was at home relaxing on the couch and I heard my parents' car pull up in the driveway, I'd panic, jump off the couch, and try to look busy before they opened the door. Exactly like I'd just seen Abby do.

That's when I stopped looking at Abby and thinking: *What is my anger telling me about her?* And started asking: *What is my anger telling me about me?* My anger was delivering a package with one of my root beliefs in it—a belief that was programmed into me during childhood: *Resting is laziness, and laziness is disrespect. Worthiness and goodness are earned with hustle.*

When Abby rested right in front of me—*outside family-designated and approved resting times*—she was challenging that root belief. She was activating it, unearthing it, bringing it into the light where I could see it. But unlike my root belief about honesty and fidelity, I didn't like this one. It didn't feel true to me. Because when I looked at Abby relaxing, my anger was almost a *bitter yearning*.

Must be nice.

Must be nice to rest in the middle of the damn day.

Must be nice to feel worthy of the space you take up on the earth without hustling to earn it every minute.

Must be nice to rest and still feel worthy.

I want to be able to rest and still feel worthy, too.

I didn't want to change Abby. I wanted to change my belief about worthiness.

Anger rings our bell and delivers one of our root beliefs. This is good information, but the next part is more than informative, it's transformational: All of the beliefs that anger delivers come with a return label.

There is a sticker on the package that says, "Here is one of your root beliefs! Would you like to keep, return, or exchange this one?"

I looked hard at the root belief about worthiness that my anger at Abby had delivered to me. I thought: *No. I don't want to keep this one. It was inherited by me, not created by me. I have outgrown it. It is no longer my truest, most beautiful belief about worthiness. I know better than this belief. It's harsh, and it's hurting me and my marriage. I don't want to pass this one down to my kids. But I don't want to return it, either. I want to exchange it for this amended one:*

Hard work is important. So are play and nonproductivity. My worth is tied not to my productivity but to my existence. I am worthy of rest.

Changing my root belief about worthiness has changed my life. I sleep a little bit later. I schedule in time for reading and walks and yoga, and sometimes (on the weekend), I even watch a TV show in the middle of the day. It's heavenly. It's also an ongoing process: Still, when I see Abby relaxing, my knee-jerk reaction is annoyance. But then I check myself. I think: *Why am I activated here? Oh, yes, that old belief. Oh, wait, never mind. I've exchanged that one.* And when Abby asks, "What's wrong?" I can say, "Nothing, honey," and mean it, mostly.

Anger delivers our boundaries to us. Our boundaries deliver our beliefs to us. Our beliefs determine how we experience the world. So even though it can be scary, we'd be wise to answer the door.

heartbreak

After a decade of listening to women, I'm convinced that our deepest fears are:

1. Living without ever finding our purpose
2. Dying without ever finding true belonging

Again and again women ask me, "How do I find my purpose? How do I find my people?"

My best advice: When heartbreak rings, answer the door.

This is what it sounds like to refuse to answer the door:

I wish I could learn more about that injustice . . . I wish I could visit that sick friend . . . I wish I could get involved with that cause . . . I wish I could read that article . . . I wish I could show up for that family . . . but I can't bear to because it'll break my heart.

It's like we really believe that our hearts were meant to be kept hidden away, bubble-wrapped, and under lockdown. As though the point of life is to *not be moved*. That's not the point. When we let ourselves be moved, we discover what moves us. Heartbreak is not something to be avoided; it's something to pursue. Heartbreak is one of the greatest clues of our lives.

The magic of heartbreak is that each person's doorbell rings in response to something specific. What rings your bell? Is it racial injustice? Bullying? Animal cruelty? Hunger? War? The environment? Kids with cancer? What is it that affects you so deeply that whenever you encounter it, you feel the need to look away? Look there. Where is the pain in the world that you just cannot stand? Stand there. The thing that breaks your heart is the very thing you were born to help heal. Every world changer's work begins with a broken heart.

I met a group of women in Iowa who'd each lost a baby to stillbirth or early infant death. They formed a sisterhood, and together, through education and other kinds of support, they've contributed to lowering the stillbirth rate in their state so significantly that doctors are scratching their heads in disbelief and gratitude. Instead of withdrawing or disconnecting from their suffering, they ran straight toward it. Their shared pain became their bond and their fuel. Now, together, they are saving others from the very heartbreak that brought them together.

Heartbreak delivers your purpose. If you are brave enough to accept that delivery and seek out the people doing that particular world-changing work, you find your people. There is no bond like the bond that is forged among people who are united in the same world-healing work.

Despair says, "The heartbreak is too overwhelming. I am too sad and too small, and the world is too big. I cannot do it all, so I will do nothing."

Courage says, "I will not let the fact that I cannot do everything keep me from doing what I can."

We all want purpose and connection.

Tell me what breaks your heart, and I'll point you toward both.

grief

Fourteen years ago, I was sitting in my sister's bedroom in the home she shared with her then husband. Tish, just a few months old, lay in her car seat on the hardwood floor, sucking on her fingers and gurgling. Sister and I were quiet. She and her husband were struggling in their marriage, and it was all quite confusing and difficult.

While we sat there, her phone pinged and she looked down at it. Then she dropped the phone and slid from her chair to the floor. I grabbed the phone from the floor and saw that her husband had just emailed that their marriage was over. I looked away from the phone and down at my sister, who appeared lifeless, like whatever had been keeping her alive and afloat had gone, like the leftovers of a deflated balloon. Then she began to wail. I have known my sister since moments after she took her first breath, and I had never heard her make a noise like this. Her wail was animalistic, and it made me feel afraid. I touched her, but there was no response. The three of us were in that room together, but we were not together anymore. The pain had taken my sister to a place all her own. Tish was completely still, her eyes wide and watery, stunned by the volume and intensity of the wailing. I remember wondering how a baby exposed to this much raw pain, this early, would be formed by it.

In the coming year, while the rest of the world carried on, my sister, Tish, and I became a small army trying to push together through the muck of grief. Sometimes I think that first year shaped Tish's depth and tenderness. She still becomes still, wide-eyed, and watery in the presence of another person's pain.

My sister moved out of the home she had painstakingly created for her future family and into a small guest room in my basement. I wanted to decorate it, to make it nice for her, but she resisted. She did not want to make a home inside my basement, inside her grief. She wanted to make it clear that she was just visiting this place. The only thing she hung on the wall was a small blue cross I gave her with the inscription "For I know the plans I have for you. Plans to give you hope and a future."

Every evening she'd come home from work, eat dinner with us, and do her best to smile and play with the kids. Then she'd walk downstairs to her room for the night. One evening, I followed her downstairs and stood outside her door. As I prepared to knock, I heard her crying softly. That is when I realized that where she was, I could not go. Grief is a lonely basement guest room. No one, not even your sister, can join you there.

So I sat down on the floor with my back against her bedroom door. I used all I had, my body and my presence, to hold vigil, to guard her process, to place myself between her and anything else that might disturb or hurt her. I stayed there for hours. I came back to her door for that nightly vigil for a very long time.

A year later, my sister left that room and walked up the stairs and out the front door of our home. Soon after, she left her job as a corporate lawyer and moved to Rwanda to help prosecute child sex offenders and return land stolen from widows. I watched her go with fear and awe. Then I watched her return to marry a man who cherishes her, with whom she'd build her true and beautiful family.

Sometimes, in the years that followed, I'd walk downstairs, stare at the door to that basement guest room, and think: *It's like that small, dark room was a cocoon. All that time she was in there undergoing a complete metamorphosis.*

Grief is a cocoon from which we emerge new.

Last year Liz's beloved partner became very sick and started dying. I was far away, so each day I would send her messages that said, "I am sitting outside your door."

One day, my mom called and asked, "How is Liz?"

I thought for a moment about how to answer. I realized I couldn't because she'd asked me the wrong question.

I said, "Mama, I think the question is not 'How is Liz?' The question is 'Who is Liz? Who will she be when she emerges from this grief?'"

Grief shatters.

If you let yourself shatter and then you put yourself back together, piece by piece, you wake up one day and realize that you have been completely reassembled. You are whole again, and strong, but you are suddenly a new shape, a new size. The change that happens to people who really sit in their pain—

whether it's a sliver of envy lasting an hour or a canyon of grief lasting decades—it's revolutionary. When that kind of transformation happens, it becomes impossible to fit into your old conversations or relationships or patterns or thoughts or life anymore. You are like a snake trying to fit back into old, dead skin or a butterfly trying to crawl back into its cocoon. You look around and see everything freshly, with the new eyes you have earned for yourself. There is no going back.

Perhaps the only thing that makes grief any easier is to surrender completely to it. To resist trying to hold on to a single part of ourselves that existed before the doorbell rang. Sometimes to live again, we have to let ourselves die completely. We have to let ourselves become completely, utterly, new.

When grief rings: Surrender. There is nothing else to do. The delivery is utter transformation.

invaders

When I began recovery, I thought that my problem was that I ate, drank, and drugged too much. I learned that overeating, drinking, and drugging were actually not my problems; they were my ineffective solutions. My actual problems are clinical depression and anxiety. Being both depressed and anxious is a bit like being Eeyore and Tigger at the same time. It's like always living a little too low and a little too high. It's always struggling to be at the level where life happens, which is here and now.

Depression and anxiety are not feelings. Feelings return me to myself. Depression and anxiety are body snatchers that suck me out of myself so that I appear to be there but I'm really gone. Other people can still see me, but no one can *feel* me anymore—including me. For me, the tragedy of mental illness is not that I'm sad but that I'm not anything. Mental illness makes me miss my own life.

Depression, for me, is a forgetting, an erasing, a slow fade into nothingness. It is like I run out of Glennon, and there is nothing left but panic that I am gone forever this time. Depression takes all my vibrant colors and bashes them together until I am gray, gray, gray. Eventually I get too low to operate, but as I begin to fade, I can usually still accomplish small things: do the dishes, take the kids to school, smile when it seems called for. It's just that it's all forced. I am acting instead of responding, because I have forgotten the point. Perhaps this is why so many depressed people become artists, to reclaim the power of answering the question: *What is the point?* We are clawing at the ground with pen and paper while drowning in quicksand.

If depression feels like sinking below, anxiety is a shaky hovering above. Right now, as I write this, I am in the middle of an anxious period that has lasted a few weeks. I know I'm floating into anxiety when I find myself obsessing. Obsessing over the next speech, the kids, the house, my marriage, my body, my hair. Anxiety is feeling terrified about my lack of control over *anything,* and obsessing is my antidote. Writing is clawing the ground when I'm sinking too low, and obsessing is clawing the ground when I'm hovering too high.

I thought I'd been hiding my anxiety until my wife touched my arm and said, "I miss you. You've been gone for a while." Of course, we've been by each other's side virtually nonstop. It's just that living with anxiety—living *alarmed*—makes it impossible to enter the moment, to land inside my body and *be* there. I cannot be in the moment because I am too afraid of what the next moment will bring. I have to be ready.

The other day a friend was describing getting a cavity filled at the dentist and she said, "It's not even the pain I hate the most—it's the anticipation of the pain. I'm sweating, panicking, waiting for it to hurt terribly bad. It never does, but it feels like it's always about to." I said, "Yes. That is how I feel all the time."

When one lives in a state of constant vigilance, if something actually goes wrong: Forget about it. Full panic. Fifteen to a hundred in two seconds flat.

Kids two minutes late?

Everyone is dead.

Sister doesn't text me back within thirty seconds?

Definitely dead.

Dog coughs?

Almost dead.

Abby's plane delayed?

Yep, all this was too good to be true, life will never let me be happy, all the death.

The good news is that I've figured out many ways to outsmart the body snatchers. Proof of my expertise in this area? I am a clinically depressed inspirational speaker. I am a diagnosed anxious person whose main job is to convince people that everything's okay. Please note that if I can be these things, anyone can be anything.

five pro tips for those who live too high and too low

1. TAKE YOUR DAMN MEDS

I am on Lexapro, and I believe it to be—along with all the personal growth shit—the reason I don't have to self-medicate with boxes of wine and Oreos anymore.

My favorite song goes like this: "Jesus loves me, this I know, for he gave me Lexapro."

Once, while playing a family game, Chase read this question to my then husband: "If you were going to be stranded on an island, who is the one person you'd bring with you?"

Craig said, "Your mom."

Chase said, "Okay. What is the one item you would bring?"

Craig said, "Your mom's meds."

I do not believe that when we die, one of us will be presented with the She Who Suffered Most trophy. If this trophy *does* exist, I don't want it. If there are people in your life—parents, siblings, friends, writers, spiritual "gurus"—who judge you for taking prescribed medicine, please ask to see their medical license. If they can show it to you and they happen to be your doctor, consider listening. If not, tell them sweetly to fuck all the way off. They are two-legged people who are calling prosthetics a crutch. They cannot go with you into the dark. Go about your business, which is to suffer less so you can live more.

2. KEEP TAKING YOUR DAMN MEDS

After you take your meds for a while, you will likely begin to feel better. You will wake up one morning, look at your pills, and think: *What was I thinking? I am a perfectly normal human, after all! I don't need those things anymore!*

Going off meds because you feel better is like standing in a torrential rainstorm holding a trusty umbrella that is keeping you toasty and dry and thinking: *Wow. I'm so dry. It's probably time to get rid of this silly umbrella.*

Stay dry and alive.

3. TAKE NOTES

This is what happens to us: We are in our homes, and we start sinking down, down, down or floating up, up, and away. We are fading and freaking out. We are in the bad part. So we make an appointment with our doctor for help. Our appointment is in a few days. We wait.

We start to feel a little bit better, day by day. The morning of our appointment, as we shower and get into the car, we can't even remember who we were or what we felt like three days ago. So we look at the doctor and think: *My down self is impos-*

sible to explain. I barely remember her. Was that even real? We end up saying something like "I don't know. I get sad. I guess everyone does. I'm fine now, I guess." Then we leave, without help.

A few days later we are in our homes. And we start sinking and floating again. And so forth.

When you start sinking into the gray, get out your phone or a notebook and write a few notes from your Down Self to your Up Self. Write about how you feel right now. This does not need to be a novel, just a note. Here is one of my notes from my Down Self:

> *It's all gray.*
> *I can't feel.*
> *I am all alone.*
> *No one knows me.*
> *I'm too tired to write any more.*

Put your note away in a safe place, and then call for that appointment. When you go to your appointment, bring your note from your Down Self. When you sit down with the doctor, you don't need to remember or translate. You just need to say, "Hello. This is me, all showered and 'fine' looking. I don't need help for this Up version of me; I need help for *this* version of me." Take out your note and hand it over. This is how you take care of your Down Self. This is one way to become her friend and advocate.

When you've been returned to yourself, write yourself another note.

Months ago, I threw away my umbrella because I was dry. Two weeks later, I'd just finished snapping at the kids for the millionth time and my people were looking at me sideways with scared eyes. I was going through the motions, making lunches, writing words. I just couldn't remember the point of these motions anymore. I realized I was gone again. But I also felt confused. *Maybe this is just who I am, actually. I can't remember.*

So I went to my jewelry box and pulled out the note my Up Self had written to me.

> G,
>
>> *You love your life (mostly).*
>> *The smell of Tish's hair makes you melt.*
>> *Sunsets blow your mind. Every time.*
>> *You laugh twenty times a day.*
>> *You see more magic than the average bear.*
>> *You feel loved. You are loved. You have a beautiful life that*
> *you have fought hard for.*
> —G

I called my doctor, got back on my meds, and returned myself to me.

Take good care of all of your selves. Fight like hell to keep yourself, and when you lose her, do whatever it takes to return to her.

4. KNOW YOUR BUTTONS

My commitment to sobriety is about staying with myself. I don't want to abandon myself ever again. Not for long, at least.

Remember those Staples commercials from a few years ago? A group of people in an office would get stressed about something, and a red "easy" button would appear out of nowhere. Someone would press that button, and the whole office would be transported out of their stress and into a pain-free place.

"Easy" buttons are the things that appear in front of us that we want to reach for because they temporarily take us out of our pain and stress. They do not work in the long run, because what they actually do is help us abandon ourselves. "Easy" buttons take us to fake heaven. Fake heaven always turns out to be hell. You know you've hit an "easy" button when, afterward, you feel more lost in the woods than you did before you hit it. It has taken me forty years to decide that when I feel bad, I want to do something that makes me feel better instead of worse.

I keep a handwritten poster in my office titled "Easy Buttons and Reset Buttons."

On the left are all the things I do to abandon myself.

On the right are my reset buttons, the things I can do to make staying with myself a little more possible.

EASY BUTTONS	RESET BUTTONS
Boozing	Drink a glass of water.
Bingeing	Take a walk.
Shopping	Take a bath.
Snarking	Practice yoga.
Comparing	Meditate.
Reading mean reviews	Go to the beach and watch the waves.
Inhaling loads of sugar and passing out	Play with my dog.
	Hug my wife and kids.
	Hide the phone.

My reset buttons are just little things. Big thinking is the kryptonite of high and low folks like me. When everything is terrible and I hate my life and I feel certain that I need a new career, a new religion, a new house, a new life, I look at my list and remember that what I really need is probably a glass of water.

5. REMEMBER THAT WE ARE THE BEST PEOPLE

I'm an artist and an activist, so pretty much *all* my friends struggle with what our culture has defined as mental illness. These people are the most alive, passionate, kind, fascinating, and intelligent humans on Earth. They live different kinds of lives than the type we're trained to aspire to. Many of them live lives that include spending days in the dark without leaving their homes and holding on to words and policy and paintbrushes for hope and dear life. This kind of life is not easy, but it's often deep, true, meaningful, and beautiful. I have begun to notice that I don't even *enjoy* folks who aren't at least a tad mentally ill. I don't wish folks without a little anxiety or depression any harm, I just don't find myself particularly curious about them. I have come to believe that we "crazies" are the best people.

This is why so many of us are resistant to taking our medication. Because deep underneath, we believe that we are actually the sane ones. We mentally ill are the only "sick" people who believe our magic is inside our disease. I did. I still do. When people said "Get better," I heard: *Get the same as everyone else*. I knew I was supposed to hang my head and declare that my way of being was dangerous and wrong and everyone else's way was better and right. I was supposed to get fixed, join the troops, and fall into line. Sometimes I desperately wanted that, because living my way was so hard. Sometimes I could make myself accept that my inability to live lightly and pleasantly in the world I'd been born into was chemical and that I needed help integrating like everybody else does. I needed to say "Uncle" and admit: *It's not you, world—it's me. I'll get help. I need to get better. I need your science.*

But other times—when I turn on the news or watch closely how people treat each other—I raise my eyebrows and think: *Actually, maybe it's not me. Maybe it's you, world. Maybe my inabil-*

ity to adapt to the world is not because I'm crazy but because I'm paying attention. Maybe it's not insane to reject the world as it is. Maybe the real insanity is surrendering to the world as it is. Maybe pretending that things around here are just fine is no badge of honor I want to wear. Maybe it's exactly right to be a little crazy. Maybe the truth is: World, you need my poetry.

I've got these conditions—anxiety, depression, addiction—and they almost killed me. *But they are also my superpowers.* The sensitivity that led me to addiction is the same sensitivity that makes me a really good artist. The anxiety that makes it difficult to exist in my own skin also makes it difficult to exist in a world where so many people are in so much pain—and that makes me a relentless activist. The fire that burned me up for the first half of my life is the exact same fire I'm using now to light up the world.

Don't forget: We need their science because they need our poetry. We don't need to be more pleasant, normal, or convenient, we just need to be ourselves. We need to save ourselves because we need to save the world.

comfort zones

I used to stay brokenhearted like it was my job and destiny. Like pain was what I owed to the world and staying sad was how I stayed safe. Self-denial was how I earned my worthiness, my goodness, my right to exist. Suffering was my comfort zone. I decided, at forty years old, to try a new way.

I chose Abby. I chose my own joy. I chose to believe—as Mary Oliver promised—that I don't have to be good, I can just let the soft animal of my body love what it loves.

I made this choice out of love for myself and Abby and also out of curiosity. I wondered if joy had as much to teach me as pain did. If so, I wanted to know.

I am not sure what the path of joy will teach me in the long run. Choosing joy is new for me. But I've learned this much: It's nice to be happy. I feel lighter and clearer and stronger and more alive. I haven't been struck down yet. One thing that has surprised me is this: The happier I become, the happier my children seem to become. I am unlearning everything I've been trained to believe about motherhood and martyrdom. In our wedding book, my son wrote, "Abby: Before you came, mom never turned our volume up past 11. Thank you." I hope that my new belief that love should make you feel both held and free is a belief my children will keep.

I've also learned that while choosing joy makes it easier for me to love myself and my life, it seems to make it harder for the world to love me.

I was speaking at an event recently, and a woman stood up in the audience, looked at me onstage, and said into the microphone, "Glennon, I used to love your writing so much. When you talked about your pain and how hard life was, I felt so comforted. But lately, with your new life, you seem different. I have to be honest: I am finding you harder and harder to relate to."

"Yes," I said. "I understand.

"I'm happier now. I'm not doubting myself as much, and that is making me confident and stronger, so I'm suffering less. I have noticed that it seems easier for the world to love a suffering woman than it is for the world to love a joyful, confident woman."

It's hard for me, too.

I was at one of Tish's soccer games, and there was a girl on the other team who was just rubbing me the wrong way. I could tell by the sideline body language and eye rolling that she was also rubbing several of my soccer-mom friends the wrong way. I watched her carefully, trying to figure out why this girl was activating us. I noticed that she walked with her head held high and with a bit of a swagger. She was good, and she knew it. She went in for the ball often and hard, like a girl who knows her own strength and talent. She smiled the whole time, like all of this was easy for her, like she was having the time of her life. All of this just annoyed the hell out of me.

She was *twelve*.

I sat with my feelings and I realized: The knee-jerk reaction I'm having to this girl is a direct result of my training. I have been conditioned to mistrust and dislike strong, confident, happy girls and women. We all have. Studies prove that the more powerful, successful, and happy a man becomes, the more people trust and like him. But the more powerful and happy a woman becomes, the less people like and trust her. So we proclaim: *Women are entitled to take their rightful place!* Then, when a woman does take her rightful place, our first reaction is: *She's so . . . entitled.* We become people who say of confident women, "I don't know, I can't explain it—it's just something about her. I just don't like her. I can't put my finger on why."

I can put my finger on why: It's because our training is kicking in through our subconscious. Strong, happy, confident girls and women are breaking our culture's implicit rule that girls should be self-doubting, reserved, timid, and apologetic. Girls who are bold enough to break those rules *irk* us. Their brazen defiance and refusal to follow directions make us want to put them back into their cage.

Girls and women sense this. We want to be liked. We want to be trusted. So we downplay our strengths to avoid threatening anyone and invoking disdain. We do not mention our accomplishments. We do not accept compliments. We temper, qualify, and discount our opinions. We walk without swagger, and we yield incessantly. We step out of the way. We say, "I feel like" instead of "I know." We ask if our ideas make sense instead of assuming they do. We apologize for . . . *everything*. Conversations among brilliant women often devolve into competitions for who wins the trophy for hottest mess. We want to be respected, but we want to be loved and accepted even more.

I once sat with Oprah Winfrey at her kitchen table, and she asked me what I was most proud of in my life as an activist, writer, mother. I panicked and started mumbling something like

"Oh. I don't feel proud, I feel grateful. None of it's really me. I'm surrounded by great people. I'm just incredibly lucky and . . ."

She put her hand on mine and said, "Don't do that. Don't be modest. Dr. Maya Angelou used to say, 'Modesty is a learned affectation. You don't want modesty, you want humility. Humility comes from inside out.'"

I think of what she said to me every day. She was saying: Playing dumb, weak, and silly is a disservice to yourself and to me and to the world. Every time you pretend to be less than you are, you steal permission from other women to exist fully. Don't mistake modesty for humility. Modesty is a giggly lie. An act. A mask. A fake game. We have no time for it.

The word *humility* derives from the Latin word *humilitas,* which means "of the earth." To be humble is to be grounded in knowing who you are. It implies the responsibility to become what you were meant to become—to grow, to reach, to fully bloom as high and strong and grand as you were created to. It is not honorable for a tree to wilt and shrink and disappear. It's not honorable for a woman to, either.

I've never pretended to be stronger than I am, so I'm sure as hell not going to pretend I'm weaker than I am. I'm also going to quit requiring modesty from other women. I don't want to find comfort in the weakness and pain of other women. I want to find inspiration in the joy and success of other women. Because that makes me happier, and because if we keep disliking and tearing down strong women instead of loving them, supporting them, and voting for them, we won't have any strong women left.

When I see a joyful, confident woman moving through the world with swagger, I'm going to forgive myself for my first reaction because it's not my fault, it's just my conditioning.

First reaction: *Who the hell does she think she is?*

Second reaction: *She knows she's a goddamn cheetah. Halle-fucking-lujah.*

elmer's

I've always judged harshly my parenting generation's obsession with their kids' sports. I've pitied the parents who spend their weekends and paychecks carting their kids all over the country to watch them kick balls or do handsprings. Each time a friend tells me about the scholarship her kid got to college, I say, "That's wonderful!" and I think: *But didn't you spend at least that much on leotards and shin guards and hotels?* For a very long while, my athletic goal for my children was mediocrity. I wanted them to learn enough about sports to avoid embarrassing themselves in gym class but not enough to become talented and ruin my weekends.

When the girls were young, they wanted to try gymnastics, so we drove to the local gym once a week and they rolled around and pointed their toes while I read and periodically looked up to yell, "Nice, honey!" This was a perfect scenario until the coach approached me after practice and said, "Your girls show real promise. It's time for them to start coming three times a week." I looked at her, smiled, thanked her, and thought: *Time for a new sport!* The following week, we joined the soccer house league. The girls had fun, and since there was zero pressure or real learning, I felt confident that we could continue to meet our mediocrity goal.

After the divorce, Tish began to fade. I watched her slowly retreat into food for comfort and spend more and more time alone in her room. I knew she needed to move her body more, but I also know, from personal experience, that suggesting this to a child will backfire. Tish was ten. I was ten when I fell into bulimia. My baby looked like she was teetering—right on the edge of falling. I was afraid.

I sat on the couch with Abby one night and said, "I think we need to get her back into therapy."

Abby said, "I disagree. I think she needs to get out of her head, not deeper into it. I've been thinking about this a lot. I want Tish to try out for an elite travel soccer team."

ME: I'm sorry. What did you just say? Have you *met* Tish? That child would not run if the house were on fire. And those travel girls have been playing since birth. No, thank you. We are trying to *help* her, not humiliate her.

ABBY: I've got a hunch here. She's a natural leader. She gets this spark in her eye when we talk about soccer. I think she might love it.

ME: No chance. She's way too fragile right now. What if she doesn't make it and it breaks her?

ABBY: What if she *makes* it and it *makes* her?

Behind my back, Abby called Craig, a lifelong soccer player, and it quickly became two against one. The plan was to approach Tish and ask if she'd like to try out for an elite travel soccer team against my will and better mama judgment. One day after school all three of us sat Tish down.

She froze and looked warily at us. After a divorce, kids are in fight-or-flight mode for a long while. She asked, "What happened? More bad news?"

Craig said, "No. No more bad news. We're wondering if you'd be interested in trying out for a travel soccer team."

Tish giggled. We didn't giggle with her, so she stopped. She looked at Craig, then me. Then her eyes locked on Abby.

TISH: Wait. Are you serious?
ABBY: Yes.
TISH: Do you think I could actually make it?

I opened my mouth to say, "Well, honey, the truth is that these girls have been playing much longer than you have and don't forget that just trying out is so brave and we will not focus on outcome, just our input . . ."

But before I could speak Abby looked Tish dead in the eyes and said, "Yes. I believe you could make it. You have potential and passion. Somebody's got to make it. Why *not* you?"

Oh my God, I thought. She is reckless. She has no fucking idea what she is doing.

Without taking her eyes off Abby, Tish said, "Okay. I'll try."

"Awesome," Craig said.

"Cool," Abby said.

DANGER AHEAD, I thought.

We three smiled at Tish.

Tryouts were four weeks away. Tish, Abby, and Craig spent those weeks at the elementary school practicing shooting and in our living room watching old Women's National Team games.

Abby and Craig traded texts and emails about training strategy. Tish and Abby talked about the game so incessantly that Soccer became the official second language of our home. They also went for runs together each day, which never went smoothly. Tish complained and cried the whole way through. One afternoon they walked into the foyer together, sweating and panting. Tish continued her run right up the stairs, stomping the entire way. Before she slammed the door to her room she screamed, "I CAN'T DO IT! I HATE IT! I CAN'T DO THIS!"

I froze and began to consider what medications we might prescribe Tish after this dangerous experiment failed and we had officially ruined her life. Again.

Abby turned me toward her and looked into my eyes. "It's fine," she said. She pointed upstairs. "That? That's exactly right. Don't go up there. She'll be down in a bit."

Tish came downstairs in a bit, red-eyed and quiet. She sat on the couch between Abby and me. We watched TV for a while, and during a commercial break Abby said, without taking her eyes off the TV, "I hated running every single day of my career. I cried about it all the time. I did it because I knew I couldn't be great if I wasn't fit, but I freaking hated every minute of it."

Tish nodded and asked, "When are we running tomorrow?"

The weeks pass, and now we are driving Tish to her first day of tryouts. I have both my hands wrapped around a gigantic travel mug filled with stress-relief tea. When we arrive at the fields, all the other girls are in their shiny travel uniforms and Tish is in a summer camp T-shirt and PE shorts. She is also at least a foot shorter than all of the other girls. When I point this out to Abby, she says, "What? No, she's not. Babe, when it

comes to Tish, you've got some kind of projected body dys-
morphia. Look closely, she's as tall as the rest of them." I squint
and say, "Hm. Well she's littler *inside*." Abby says, "No, she's
not, Glennon. No. She's not."

Tish, Abby, Craig, and I huddle up. Tish looks at me, and
her eyes are watery. I hold my breath. Abby looks at me and
widens her eyes. I want to say, "Baby, let's forget about all of
this. Mommy's got you. Let's get back in that car and go get
some ice cream." Instead I say, "I believe in you, Tish. This is a
hard thing to do. We can do hard things."

She turns away from us and begins to move slowly toward
the field. I watch her walk away from me and toward this very,
very hard thing and never in my life has my heart traveled so far
up my throat. She looks so small, and the sky, field, and task
ahead of her are so big. She keeps walking, though, away from
us, toward the sideline bench where the other girls are sitting.
As soon as she makes it to the bench, she and we realize: Oh my
God. Oh my God—there is no room left on the bench for her.
She stands awkwardly off to the side. She doesn't know what to
do with her hands. She is on the fringe. She is outside the
Golden circle. She does not belong. She is not one of them.

Abby grabs my hand. "You okay?"

ME: No. This is a mistake.
ABBY: This is not a mistake.

I grab my hand back and pray: *Please, God, if you exist, make
them be nice to my daughter. Make them invite her into the circle. Make
the ball go into the goal every time she touches it or just create some other
kind of soccer miracle so she'll somehow make this team. If all else fails,
send an earthquake. But please, God, let this be over soon, because my
heart cannot take this.*

Tryouts begin. Tish doesn't seem to know what she's doing.

She loses the ball often. She isn't as quick as the other girls. She looks over at Abby several times, and Abby smiles and nods at her. Tish keeps trying. She has a few good moments. She can complete a pass, and Abby insists that she has some kind of vision of the field, an understanding of the game that seems to exceed the other girls' vision. But the hour is tough on her. And me. After it's over, we walk to the car together and climb in. Tish is quiet the whole way home. After a while I turn around and say, "Baby?"

Abby puts her hand on mine and shakes her head no. I turn back around and stay quiet the rest of the way home.

We go back to tryouts the next day. And the next. We go back every night for a week. On Friday night, we get an email from the coach. It says, "She's got a lot to learn. But she's got a spark and she's a hard worker and a leader. We need that. We'd like to offer Tish a spot on our team."

I cover my mouth and reread the email twice to make sure I'm understanding it correctly. Abby is doing the same thing silently over my shoulder. I turn around to her and say, "Holy. *Shit*. How did you know?"

Abby has tears in her eyes. She says, "I didn't know. I haven't slept through the night for three weeks."

Craig, Abby, and I sit Tish down and tell her together.

"You made it," we say. "You made the team."

It's been a few years since those tryouts, and now we are parents who spend our weekends carting our child all over the state and spend our money on gas and hotels and tournaments and cleats.

Tish is strong and solid now, not because she wants to be a model, but because she wants to be the best athlete and teammate she can be. The stronger she is, the more her team can count on her. Tish does not consider her body an end in itself, but a means to an end. She uses her body as a tool to help her achieve a goal her mind and heart have set: *Win games with my friends*.

Tish is a leader now. She has learned that there are great athletes and there are great teammates, and they are not always the same people. She watches her teammates, and she decides exactly what each needs. She knows who is hurting and who needs encouragement. After every game, win or lose, she sits in the back seat on the drive home and sends her teammates messages: "It's okay, Livvie. Nobody could have stopped that ball. We'll get them next time. We love you." The girls' parents write me emails saying, "Please thank Tish for me. She was the only one who could console my girl."

Tish is an athlete now. When drama hits at middle school, it doesn't shake her badly because those hallways are not where she finds her identity. She doesn't need to manufacture false drama in her social life because she has all the real drama—the thrill of victory and the agony of defeat—on the pitch. The other day I heard her say this to a friend of Chase's: "Nah, I'm not popular. I'm a soccer player."

Soccer saved my daughter.

The fact that I didn't save my daughter from soccer saved my daughter.

Recently, Craig, Abby, and I sat on the sidelines in the cold, pouring rain and watched Tish's team play. The girls were soaking and freezing and somehow showed zero signs of being either one. I watched Tish closely, as always. Her legs and face were both chiseled. Her hot-pink pre-wrap headband held back strays from her signature ponytail. The other team had just scored, and she was trying to catch her breath and get back into position. As she ran, she called back to her defenders, "Let's go. We've got this!" Play resumed. The ball came to Tish. She trapped the ball and passed it to her forward, Anais. Anais scored.

The girls ran toward Anais, toward each other. They all met in the center of the field, a mass of tween girls leaping and hugging and celebrating each other, their team, their sweat. We parents cheered, too, but the girls didn't hear us. In that moment, there was no one else on Earth but them. How we felt about them didn't matter. How they felt was what mattered. For them, it was not a performance. It was real.

The game ended, and Abby, Craig, and I walked to our cars, parked side by side. We all climbed inside to get out of the rain. After a quick team huddle, Tish walked toward us with her friend Syd. They were not hurrying, because they didn't even feel the cold. When they got to us, they hugged, and Syd walked off with her mom. Tish came over and stood outside Abby's window to say good-bye because she was going home with Craig. It's still tough, all this back-and-forth between houses. Divorce is hard to navigate—all families are hard to navigate—but Tish knows that she can do hard things.

The rain continued to fall around her, but Tish's face was a floodlight framed by the window.

She said, "Coach Mel gave me a nickname today. She says she's going to call me Elmer's because the ball sticks to me like glue. When she called me off the bench today, she yelled, 'Elmer's—you're in.'"

Craig's window was open, and he heard her story. He smiled over at me and Abby. We smiled back. Tish just stood there between us—glowing and gluing.

luckies

When Abby and I first fell in love, we had hundreds of miles and a million obstacles keeping us apart. The facts laid out in front of us made a future together seem impossible. So we'd tell each other about the true and beautiful unseen order we felt pressing through our skin. Our imaginings always included each other and the water.

Abby wrote this to me from the other coast, one evening before she fell asleep:

"It's early in the morning and I'm sitting on our dock watching the sunrise. I look and see you in your pajamas, still sleepy, walking toward me, holding two mugs of coffee. We just sit there on the dock together, my back against the piling, your back against my chest, watching the fish jump and the sun rise. We have nowhere to be but together."

The harder things became, the more often we'd return to that morning Abby had imagined for us. That dock, her, me, two steaming mugs of coffee: That image became our unseen order, guiding us forward. We had faith.

A year later, Abby made dinner for the six of us: the kids, Craig, and me. We all sat down to eat on the back porch of the home off the Gulf of Mexico that Abby and I bought together. It was a gorgeous evening, the sky all purples and oranges and the breeze steady and warm. We ate and laughed and then cleared the table together. Craig left for his Sunday-evening soccer game, and the kids finished the dishes and then sat down on the couch to watch a show. Honey, our bulldog, snuggled up on Amma's lap, and Abby walked outside to our dock: the Doyle Melton Wamdock. I watched from inside as she sat down with her back against a piling and looked out at the canal. I poured two hot teas and walked out to join her. She looked back toward me, and by her smile, I knew she was remembering. We sat on the dock together, my back against her chest, her back against the piling, and we watched the fish jump while the sun set and the sky celebrated in deeper and deeper purples.

Before we went back inside, I snapped a picture of us, smiling with the sun setting behind us, and later I posted it. Someone commented, "Gah. You're so lucky to have each other and this life."

I replied, "It's true. We are terribly lucky. It is also true that we imagined this life before it existed and then we each gave up everything for the one-in-a-million chance that we might be able to build it together. We did not fall into this world we have now, we made it. I'll tell you this: *The braver I am, the luckier I get*."

buzzes

I used to hate romantic movies. When they came on the television, I'd feel achy, like I was looking at pictures of a party I hadn't been invited to. I'd remind myself that romantic love is just Disney bullshit, but I'd always feel a yearning right before changing the channel.

Like the yearning that Abby, who is agnostic, feels when she watches a church choir with their robes and deep voices and shiny eyes.

I've always had shiny eyes about divine love; I'm a believer.

Abby has always had shiny eyes about romantic love; she's a believer.

Abby's favorite movies are *Romeo + Juliet* and *The Notebook*. *The NOTEBOOK*. When I say to her, "I cannot believe we found each other," she says, "I can. I knew you were out there the whole time."

I didn't know. I didn't know about romantic love because I didn't fall in love until I was forty years old. There I was, just walking down the street of my life, when I fell into a rabbit hole. This is why they call it falling in love, because there is suddenly no solid ground beneath you anymore.

When I fell in love, I felt a lot like I did when I ate hallucinogenic mushrooms with my friends in college. When the mushrooms kicked in, we'd fall into the rabbit hole together. Suddenly I'd feel utterly connected to the people I was tripping with and equally disconnected from everyone sober. My friends and I were in a bubble of love, and no one else could reach us or understand us. I felt sorry for the sober people. They didn't know what we knew or feel what we felt or love like we loved. We called them the normal people. "Be careful," we'd whisper to each other when one of them would approach. "She's normal."

For a long while, that was how I felt about everyone who was not me and Abby. I'd look at folks walking down the street and think: *They don't even know. We are special, and they are so . . . normal.* The only normal person I could even speak to during those early days was my sister. She talked to me back then exactly like she'd talked to me when I was a drunk. She'd cock her head to the side and say things like "Be careful, Sissy. You don't really know what you're doing right now."

I'd think: *Oh my gosh. She thinks this is a phase. She doesn't understand that I have found love and so now I am different and special forever. This is what I've been missing. This is why life has been hard for me: because I didn't have this one thing. Now I am better. This is who I am now. I am meandAbby.*

One night, Abby and I were sitting on the couch, wrapped around each other, kissing and talking about eloping.

Abby said, "We gotta be smart. Our brains are lit up like Christmas trees right now."

I pulled back from her. I felt confused, like one of my shrooming friends had turned to me in the middle of a trip and asked if I would help her with her taxes. I felt lonely, like Abby had abandoned me and become normal without me. I felt annoyed, like she was suggesting that our love was not personal but chemical. Like it was not magic, just science. I was under the impression that our love was the opposite of the drugs that we had used to light up our brains and escape our lives for decades. I was under the impression that we were healing each other, not drugging each other. I was under the impression that we were Juliet and Juliet, not Syd and Nancy.

Abby said, "I'm afraid for when this beginning part ends for you."

"What do you mean?"

"You've never fallen in love, so you've never been in this part before. I have. It changes. I want the change. I want the next part. I've never had that before. This first part isn't the realest part. The next part, when we stop falling together and land side by side, that's the real part. It's coming. I want it, but I'm afraid that when it comes, when we land, you'll be disappointed and you'll panic."

"I feel like you're saying that we're under some kind of spell and soon it will wear off and we will love each other less than this."

"What I'm saying is that soon the spell will wear off and we're going to need to love each other more than this."

After a few months, I started noticing that our love shrooms started wearing off. I started to see Abby as separate from me, and I started to feel myself becoming normal again. That was a tragedy for me, because I thought that she was the thing that had finally saved me from having to be myself. I thought I could just be *us* forever now. She was right. I did panic. One night I wrote her this poem:

colors

Two years ago
You were pearl white
I was midnight blue.
We became sky blue.
Pearl gone, midnight gone
All sky blue.
But now, sometimes, you go.
To a meeting, to a friend, an opinion, a show.
When you go, I'm left with me again.
You take your pearl. I feel my midnight again.
This is right, I know.
Midnight is how I make things.
I just thought, for a minute, that I was gone.
I miss being gone.
The end of the Beginning is existing again.
We will be beautiful and strong side by side.
But between you and me (between pearl and midnight)
I liked sky blue better.

I look at that poem now, and I think: *Glennon, you are always so desperate to find yourself and ready to abandon yourself. You so badly want to be seen and to disappear. You have forever been desperate to yell "HERE I AM" and to fade away at the very same time.*

Abby and I have been normal people for a couple of years now. We are in the next part now. The initial buzz has worn off, but sometimes we're sky blue again. It's not a permanent state anymore; it comes in fleeting moments. It happens when we make love, steal a kiss in the kitchen, catch each other's eyes when the kids do something amazing. Mostly, though, we're separate colors. This is a beautiful thing, because we can really see each other. I have decided that I want to be in love with a person, not a feeling. I want to be found in love, not lost in it. I'd rather exist than disappear. I'm going to be midnight forever. That's perfect.

sandcastles

Ask a woman who she is, and she'll tell you who she loves, who she serves, and what she does. *I am a mother, a wife, a sister, a friend, a career woman.* The fact that we define ourselves by our roles is what keeps the world spinning. It's also what makes us untethered and afraid. If a woman defines herself as a wife, what happens if her partner leaves? If a woman defines herself as a mother, what happens when the kids leave for college? If a woman defines herself as a career woman, what happens when the company folds? *Who we are* is perpetually being taken from us, so we live in fear instead of peace. We cling too tightly, close our eyes to what we need to look at hard, avoid questions that need to be asked, and in a million ways insist to our friends, partners, and children that the purpose of their existence is to define us. We build sandcastles and then try to live inside them, fearing the inevitable tide.

Answering the question *Who do I love?* is not enough. We must live lives of our own. To live a life of her own, each woman must also answer: *What do I love? What makes me come alive? What is beauty to me, and when do I take the time to fill up with it? Who is the soul beneath all of these roles?* Each woman must answer these questions now, before the tide comes. Sandcastles are beautiful, but we cannot live inside them. Because the tide rises. That's what the tide does. We must remember: I am the builder, not the castle. I am separate and whole, over here, eyes on the horizon, sun on my shoulders, welcoming the tide. Building, rebuilding. Playfully. Lightly. Never changing. Always changing.

guitars

It's late afternoon, and I'm winding down from a nine-hour workday. Abby pops her head into my office and says, "Babe! Guess what? I'm going to start playing ice hockey! I found a league that plays Monday nights. I'm looking at gear now. I'm so psyched."

ME: Wait. What? You play *ice hockey*?

ABBY: No, but I used to play when I was little. My brothers would put me in goal, and I'd just stand there and let the pucks bounce off of me. So fun.

Fun.

I am confused about "fun." Abby is always asking me "What do you do for fun?" I find the question aggressive. What is fun? I don't do fun. I am a grown-up. I do family, work, and trash TV. Repeat forever.

But we are newlyweds, so I am still sweet. I say, "That's great, honey!"

Abby smiles, comes over to kiss me on the cheek, then walks out the front door. I stare at my computer. I have so many questions.

Why does she get to have fun? Who has the time and money for *fun*? I'll tell you who: everyone in this family but me. Craig has soccer and Chase has photography and the girls have . . . everything. *Everyone* has a thing but me. Must be nice to have time for a *thing*.

This "must be nice" thought stops me. It always does.

Hmm. Maybe it *is* nice. Maybe that's why they all want a thing.

Maybe *I* want a thing.

I sit and think about the one thing I've always wanted to be: a rock star. I am so jealous of rock stars. If I could have one talent I do not have, it would be singing. When I was little, I used to stand in front of the mirror with a hairbrush and transform into Madonna in an arena. Now it's P!nk. In my car, alone. I am P!nk. I am the P!nkest. I am P!nker than P!nk. I am Deep Magenta.

I realize that my wife, Madonna, and P!nk have rung my doorbell and are delivering a package. I am wildly envious of all of them, and envy is the red flashing arrow pointing me toward what to do next. So, I search "guitar lessons, Naples Florida" on my phone. I follow the links. I find a guitar teacher who offers lessons to high school kids in a tiny music store a couple miles from my house. I call her. I set up a time for my first lesson.

When Abby walks back through the front door, I meet her in the foyer, alive and bouncing.

ME: Hi! Can you keep the kids on Fridays after school?
ABBY: Sure, why?
ME: I'm going to start guitar lessons. My whole life I

have wanted to be a rock star, so I am going to go ahead and be one now. I am going to learn to play the guitar, and then I am going to write my own songs, and when we are at parties I am going to pull out my guitar and people are going to gather around and sing along. They will be so happy because they were separate and lonely until my music mixed them all together. And everyone is going to think: *She is so cool.* And then I will likely get discovered and find myself on a stage somewhere singing to thousands. I won't be good at singing, I know that's what you're thinking. But that is the point! I won't be the kind of singer who inspires people because she's good, I will be the kind of singer who inspires people because she's bad! Like, people will listen to me onstage and instead of thinking: *I wish I could sing like her,* they'll think: *Well, if she can sing up there, then I guess I can do anything.*

ABBY: Okay, babe. Trying to follow all of this. You're starting guitar lessons. This is awesome. And sexy. Wait, did I hear you say that we are going to start attending *parties,* too?

ME: No.

I love learning to play guitar. It's hard, but it opens up another part of me, one that makes me feel more human. I think the word for this experience might be *fun.* But to have that fun, I had to climb down from Martyrdom Mountain. I had to allow myself one less thing to sigh about. I had to ask for help. I had to sacrifice some of my moral high ground, perhaps lose a few points in the She Who Suffers Most competition. I think we are only bitter about other people's joy in direct proportion to our commitment to keep joy from ourselves. The more often I do things I want to do, the less bitter I am at people for doing what they want to do.

I made my rock star debut on Instagram recently. I played "Every Rose Has Its Thorn," and three times as many people watched as there are seats in Madison Square Garden. I am just saying: Deep Magenta.

braids

My ex-husband has a girlfriend. Months ago, we decided it was time for us to meet. The three of us arranged to have breakfast at a local restaurant. I arrived first, sat on a bench, played with my phone, and waited. Eventually I saw the two of them approaching, and I stood up. She smiled and when we hugged, her hair smelled like a flower I couldn't identify.

We asked for a table by the water. She and Craig sat down on one side; I sat on the other and placed my purse on the seat next to me. When the waiter came, I ordered hot tea. He delivered it to the table in a little white teapot. I didn't know what else to talk about, so I talked about the little white teapot.

I said, "Look at this! How cute is this? My own teapot."

The next week, I opened a box in the mail. Inside there were two little white teapots—from her to me.

When my daughters go to their father's house, she is there with them, and she braids my daughters' hair skillfully. I have never known how to braid my daughters' hair. I've tried, but it ends up looking lumpy and pathetic, so we stick to ponytails.

Whenever I see a little girl wearing complicated braids, I think: *She looks well loved. She looks well mothered. She looks like a little girl whose mother knows what she's doing. Who once was a teenage girl who knew what she was doing, who had lots of friends in high school, who all sat around and braided each other's hair and giggled. Who was Golden.*

When Craig and his girlfriend drop the kids off at our house, we stand in the foyer together in a little circle and we are kind and awkward. I tell too many jokes and laugh too often and too loudly. We each do the best we can. Sometimes, while we're standing there, she pulls my girls over, wraps her arms around them, and plays with their hair. When this happens, Abby grabs my hand and squeezes. When Craig and his girlfriend leave, I pull my girls close again. They look well mothered, and they smell like a flower I can't identify.

The kids, Abby, and I got up early this past Thanksgiving morning, piled into the car, and drove to the Turkey Trot race downtown. On the way, Chase read us a meme that said, "My greatest fear is marrying into a family that runs Turkey Trots on Thanksgiving morning."

Craig and his girlfriend met us there. As we approached the starting line, Craig and Chase went to the front of the pack; their goal to win. Craig's girlfriend, my daughters, and I found a place in the back; our goal to finish, maybe. Abby placed herself in the middle, surveying; her goal to make sure everyone achieved their goal.

The race began. We stuck together for a while, then drifted apart. Halfway through the race, I saw Craig's girlfriend jogging ahead of me. I've always thought of "picking up the pace" as something one does metaphorically, but suddenly I felt my feet literally picking up their pace. I began to run instead of jog. I began to run strenuously. I began to run so strenuously that I felt myself sweating and panting. I began sprinting. As I approached Craig's girlfriend, I weaved to the far left so she wouldn't see me pass her. Farther along, I saw Tish running alone, but I didn't slow down; I left her in my dust. My knee started to hurt, but I didn't slow down for my knee either. I crossed the finish line having beat Craig's girlfriend. By a long stretch.

Still trying to catch my breath, I grabbed a water and walked back to the finish line to wait for my girls. I scanned the sea of runners finishing and saw Abby, Tish, Amma, and Craig's girlfriend cross the finish line together. Abby had finished early and gone back, rounded up the troops, made sure they all crossed together. They were giggling, happy, Abby on one side, Craig's girlfriend on the other, Amma and Tish in the middle. Nobody seemed to notice my absence or my victory.

A few days later, I stood in my driveway and called Craig. I said, "She tells Tish that she loves her. Don't you think that's a little much? She is your girlfriend, not their mother. We all need some boundaries. You need to help her set them. What if she leaves and hurts our kids?"

I am much more afraid that she will stay and love our kids.

We all ate Christmas dinner together this year. I asked Craig to bring the traditional apple pie. He and his girlfriend brought a strawberry dish instead. When Tish asked where the apple pie was, I shrugged and shushed her. After dinner, we took a family picture: all of us and the dog. After we took it, Craig's girlfriend said, "Okay, now let's do a crazy one!" *Why all the suggestions? We don't do crazy ones.* All three kids agreed that the crazy picture was the best picture. Then we sat down and ate the strawberry dish. All three kids said it was the best Christmas dessert we'd ever had.

The next day, Craig's girlfriend posted our crazy picture online. She wrote, "Grateful to have found a love that is inviting and kind, witty and nonjudgmental, a no boundaries type of love."

Someday I'll ask her how to braid my daughters' hair.

Someday I'll learn how to mother with her, with Abby, like a braid.

seconds

Sometimes, when heated conflict arises between Abby and me, we stop talking, take a breath and say to each other, "Okay, let's not first-marriage this. Let's second-marriage this." What we mean is: Let's not go on autopilot here. Let's use what we've learned and apply it. Let's be careful and wise and put our egos aside and remember that we are on the same team. Now that we know better, let's do better.

I would have described myself as the spiritual director of my first marriage. I had the vision for our plot, and Craig fucked it up. I now understand that this is because each person has their own plot. No one can be a supporting actor in someone else's storyline. They can pretend to, but they will always have subplots brewing inside and unfolding outside.

I am very controlling. I want to control things. This is because I am afraid. Things feel so precarious. When I was young, I made myself feel safer by controlling my food and body. I still do that. But as I got older and became a wife and a mother, I found another thing to try to control to create safety: my people. Since life is scary and precarious, controlling people I love felt like the responsible thing to do.

In addition to the fear factor, there is something else that leads me to want to control things, and that is my belief that I am very smart and creative. I really do believe I have very good ideas and that people would do best if they got on board. This kind of control is called *leadership*.

For a long while, I have controlled and led my people and called that love. I "loved" my people to a bloody pulp. My role in the lives of the people I love has been as follows: *I exist to make all your hopes and dreams come true. So let's sit down and take a look at this comprehensive list of hopes and dreams I've created for you. I have been paying very close attention and trust me, I SEE you and know you better than you know yourself. You can do anything I put your mind to! Let us begin!*

But we cannot feel and know and imagine for other people. This is what I am trying to understand. The person who is teaching me this is my wife. My wife is uncontrollable.

I love my wife more wildly than I have ever loved a grown human in my life. Before I met her, I wasn't even all that afraid of dying. Now the thought of death panics me daily, not because of death itself but because of the idea of not being with her. Death, to me, is just the ultimate FOMA: Fear of Missing Abby. Since I love Abby the most, it follows that I have to control her the most. I want to make all of my dreams for her come true. I just really want my best for her. To that end, I have relentless good ideas to share with her about what she should do and wear and eat and how she should work and sleep and read and listen. But every time I try to share my good ideas—overtly or covertly—she somehow knows what I'm doing, calls me out on it, and categorically rejects my efforts. She does this gently. She says things like "I see what you're doing there, babe. I love you for the effort, but no, thank you, I'm good."

For the first year of our marriage, I assumed that this was just a fresh, exciting challenge. I assumed that my job was to find new ways to *approach* her. Here is an actual conversation with my sister during my first year of marriage in response to the problem of Abby's continuing to insist that she was the boss of herself:

ME: Okay, I hear you, but what if I actually *know* my idea is better for her than her idea is for her? Should I just *pretend* to think her idea is good? Should I just smile and let her try her idea so we can get to mine when hers doesn't work so well? How long will I have to carry on with this time-wasting charade?

SISTER: My God. Okay. If that's how you have to think of it, Glennon, then yes, try that. Try to fake it till you make it.

So that is what I did. I just smiled and faked it. I let her lead, but only because it was my undercover leadership strategy. I decided that we would try things her way for a while, until we both saw the light *together*. For a solid year, we were spontaneous when I preferred a plan. We were trusting of people when I was skeptical. We took big risks even when I had already calculated that the odds were against us. We let the kids try things I was sure they'd fail at and then resent us for forever.

We lived, for a while, as if life were less precarious than it is, as if people were better than they are, as if our kids were tougher than I believed them to be, and as if "things generally work themselves out." It was reckless and ridiculous and irresponsible. Things do not work themselves out. I work things out. I WORK THEM OUT, and if I don't there is no working out at all. There is just chaos.

I took lots of deep breaths and started a daily yoga practice to deal with my anxiety, and I waited for things to fall apart so I could save us.

I kept waiting.

Damned if "things" didn't generally *just keep working out.* Damned if I didn't start feeling happier. Damned if our children didn't become braver, kinder, more relaxed. Damned if our life didn't get more beautiful. It was annoying as hell, honestly.

I really think that it is possible that Abby has good ideas.

I am beginning to unlearn what I used to believe about control and love. Now I think that maybe control is not love. I think that control might actually be the opposite of love, because control leaves no room for trust—and maybe love without trust is not love at all. I am beginning to play with the idea that love is trusting that other people Feel, Know, and Imagine, too. Maybe love is respecting what your people feel, trusting that *they know,* and believing that they have their own unseen order for their lives pressing through their own skin.

Maybe my role with the people I love is not imagining the truest, most beautiful life for them and then pushing them toward it. Maybe I'm just supposed to ask what they feel and know and imagine. And then, no matter how different their unseen order is from mine, ask what I can do to support *their vision.*

Trusting people is terrifying. Maybe if love is not a little scary and out of our control, then it is not love at all.

It is wild to let others be wild.

ideas

One night after dinner, Abby, Craig, my sister, her husband John, and I sat around the kitchen table for hours. Music played in the background, the kids chased Honey around the family room, and all of us sipped tea or wine and laughed until it hurt.

I pulled Honey into my lap, turned toward Craig, and said, "I want to tell you something."

Everyone at the table fell quiet.

"Do you remember that day, eighteen years ago, when we sat side by side on my front porch—me nauseous from morning sickness and you nauseous from shock—trying to decide what to do?

"Do you remember how you broke the silence?

"You said, 'I've been thinking. What if we don't get married? What if we just live separately and raise the baby side by side?'

"You knew.

"A week before I found out I was pregnant, my friend

Christy asked me how it was going with you. I said, 'We have to break up. We can't connect. Not physically, not emotionally. It's just not there.'

"I knew.

"But I had this idea—a vision of what a family should look like, what you should want, who you should become. My imagination became a dangerous thing when we let it eclipse our Knowing.

"We were so young and afraid back then. We hadn't yet learned that Knowing never goes away. It just stays there inside, solid and unmoving. It just waits as long as it takes for the snow to settle.

"I am sorry that I ignored our Knowing. We didn't fit together. We tried, because it was the right thing to do, because we thought we should. Because *I* thought we should. But right is not real, and should is a cage. What's wild is what *is*.

"Our Knowing was right all along. What *is* lasted. Because here we are: trying your idea. Being two people who were not made for each other but who are a hell of a team at raising kids side by side.

"I hope that whatever you do next is born from you and not imposed on you. I hope the rest of your life is your idea. For what it's worth, I hope you trust yourself. You know what you know. You have good ideas, Craig."

sidelines

My wife and ex-husband play on the same adult league soccer team on Wednesday nights. After dinner, we pack up the car with chairs and snacks, and the kids and I sit on the sidelines and watch their dad and their bonus mom work together to score goals.

A few weeks ago, the kids and I were sitting on the sidelines and an older couple sat down next to us. The woman pointed toward my girls and asked, "Are those your daughters?"

"They are," I said.

"Is their dad out there playing?"

"Yes, he is. That's him." I pointed to Craig.

"Where do you all live?"

"We live right here in Naples, but separately. He and I are divorced now."

"Wow, it's wonderful that you still come watch him play!"

"Yes, we love watching him play. Also, the girls' mom is playing. We come to watch her, too."

The woman looked confused. She said, "Oh! I thought you were their mom."

I said, "I am! That's their other mom."

I pointed to Abby. The woman looked closely. "Good Lord," she said. "That woman looks exactly like Abby Wambach."

"That woman *is* Abby Wambach," I said.

She said, "Wow! Your ex-husband is remarried to Abby Wambach?"

"Close! *I'm* married to Abby Wambach."

It took her a minute. A full minute of quiet. *Selah.* Old structural ideas burning, a new order of things being born inside her.

Then she smiled.

"Oh! Wow," she said.

Tish's first word was "Wow." On an early-December morning in Virginia, I pulled her out of her crib and walked her over to the nursery window. I lifted the shade, and we both saw that the backyard was covered in white. It was her first snow. Tish's eyes got big, she reached out her hand to touch the cold window, and she said, "Wow."

When people encounter our family, their eyes get big and they say "Wow"—in one tone or another—because they haven't seen a family exactly like ours before. Our family is specific, because we are specific people. We did not use a blueprint created by someone else and then struggle to fit each of us inside. We create and re-create our family again and again—from the inside of each one of us—out. We will continue to do that forever, so each of us will always have room to grow and grow and still belong. That is what family is to me: where we are both held and free.

levels

Eight years ago, I found myself in a therapist's office asking for strategies to cope with betrayal-induced rage. The therapist said, "Your anxiety is controlling you, which means that you are lost in your head. You don't know what you want. You are so disconnected. You need to remember how to get back into your body somehow."

She then suggested that I go to yoga. The next morning, on my way to the studio, I wonder: *Why did I leave my body to live in this dangerous mind of mine?* I sit on my mat in a ninety-degree room and immediately remember why.

As soon as I get still, the snow settles, and I sink into my body. I start to feel itchy and agitated and annoyed. *This is why I left!* Because I am shame and fear wrapped in skin. I don't even want to visit my body, much less reside here. But now I'm stuck: The perimeter of the yoga mat is my entire world. The other women are silent. There is nothing on the walls to read. There is no escape. *Where's my phone? There's the door. I could go. I would not have to explain.*

The instructor walks in, and I ignore her to continue plotting my escape, until she says, "Be still and know." That phrase again. I so desperately want to know. Whatever it is that I am missing, whatever it is that other people know, whatever it is that helps them cope and lets them just *live:* I want to know it.

So I stayed on that goddamn mat until I knew.

Just like I stayed in my addictions until I knew.

Just like I stayed in my marriage until I knew.

Just like I stayed in my religion until I knew.

Just like I stayed in my pain and shame until I knew.

And now I know.

I'm sitting on my couch between two friends, sipping coffee. My dog's asleep in my friend Saskia's lap. We're all listening to Ashley tell her story about staying in the hot yoga room until it made her sick. After she says, "I mean, the door wasn't even locked," the room falls quiet. Ashley has said something important. Saskia rubs the dog's head. Karyn squints her eyes. I think this:

The truth of my thirties was: *Stay on your mat, Glennon. The staying is making you.*

The truth of my forties is: *I'm made.*

I will not stay, not ever again—in a room or conversation or relationship or institution that requires me to abandon myself. When my body tells me the truth, I'll believe it. I trust myself now, so I will no longer suffer voluntarily or silently or for long. I'll look at those women to my left and right who must stay, because it's that time for them, because they have to know what love and God and freedom are *not* before they can know what love and God and freedom *are*. Because they want to know. Because they are warriors. I'll send them every bit of my strength and solidarity to help them through this part. And then I'll pick up my mat and slowly, deliberately, lightly walk out.

Because I have just remembered that the sun is shining, the breeze is cool, and these doors, they're not even locked.

human

In my favorite holy text, there is a poem about a group of people desperate to understand and define God.

They ask: *What are you?*

God says: *I am.*

They say: *You are . . . what?*

God says: *I am.*

What are you, Glennon?

Are you happy?

Are you sad?

Are you Christian?

Are you a heretic?

Are you a believer?

Are you a doubter?

Are you young?

Are you old?

Are you good?

Are you bad?

Are you dark?

Are you light?

Are you right?

Are you wrong?

Are you deep?

Are you shallow?

Are you brave?

Are you weak?

Are you shattered?

Are you whole?

Are you wise?

Are you foolish?

Are you sick?

Are you healed?

Are you lost?

Are you found?

Are you gay?

Are you straight?

Are you crazy?

Are you brilliant?

Are you caged?

Are you wild?

Are you human?

Are you alive?

Are you sure?

I am.

I am.

I am.

acknowledgments

The reason this book exists (the reason I exist) is because of the people listed here who, each day, breathe my art—and me—into existence:

ABBY: If you're a bird, I'm a bird.

CHASE: You Are Our Family's Knowing.

TISH: You Are Our Family's Feeling.

AMMA: You Are Our Family's Imagination.

CRAIG: For loving our children so masterfully, for trusting me to make art about our new family, for your humor, forgiveness, and relentless goodness.

MOM, DAD: For the patient courage that helped me find and keep myself and the love of my life. For trusting me as I learned to trust myself. I vow to give your grandchildren the same gift you give me: to live both held and free.

AMANDA: The great luck of my life is to call the kindest, bravest, most brilliant person on Earth Sister. Everything good in my life is born from that original luck. My sobriety, my family, my career, my activism, my joy, and peace: It's all because you walk in front and beside and behind me. *I am* because of you.

ALLISON: Your artistic genius is woven into every word written in here and spoken out there. All of it is *ours*. Thank you for directing so much of your talent, dedication, loyalty, and friendship my way. You are pure Gold.

DYNNA: Thank you for your brain and your heart, for your steadfast devotion to our mission and sisterhood, and for sending us to the moon.

LIZ B: Countless women and children's lives are changed because you see them, believe them, and work so relentlessly for them. I have never known someone to use her One Life with more beauty and impact than you use yours. Thank you for being Together Rising's heartbeat.

OUR TOGETHER RISING VOLUNTEERS AND WARRIORS: Katherine, Gloria, Jessica, Tamara, Karen, Nicol, Natalie, Meghan, Erin, Christine, Ashley, Lori, Kristin, Rhonda, Amanda, Meredith, and Grace—for tirelessly forging that bridge between heartbreak and action. And to Kristen B, Marie F, and Liz G—for investing your exquisite trust in our work.

WHITNEY FRICK: For being the champion, advocate, and ambassador of my work for a decade. For believing when the ideas are invisible, and for tirelessly working to help them become real.

MARGARET RILEY KING: For your tenacity, vision, humor, wisdom, and friendship.

JENNIFER RUDOLPH WALSH: For trusting in our unseen order until it became a nationwide dance party.

KATY NISHIMOTO: For your love and loyalty, and for being the quiet genius behind so many true and beautiful things.

UNCLE KEITH.

EVERYONE AT THE DIAL PRESS AND RANDOM HOUSE: For devoting your talent and passion so fully to *Untamed,* especially Gina Centrello, Avideh Bashirrad, Debbie Aroff, Michelle Jasmine, Sharon Propson, Rose Fox, Robert Siek, Christopher Brand, and the late legendary Susan Kamil. And to Scott Sherratt, for making our audiobook magic. I am elated to be on this team with all of you.

LIZ G: For being the Patron Saint of *Untamed,* a goddamn cheetah, and a believer in magic and freedom and women and me.

KARYN, JESSICA, ASHLEY: For calling me friend even though I don't leave home or text back.

KAT, EMMA: For showing me what it looks like to never become tamed in the first place.

> *Here's to The Untamed:*
> *May we know them.*
> *May we raise them.*
> *May we love them.*
> *May we read them.*
> *May we elect them.*
> *May we be them.*

ABOUT THE AUTHOR

Glennon Doyle is the author of the #1 *New York Times* best-seller *Love Warrior,* an Oprah's Book Club selection, as well as the *New York Times* bestseller *Carry On, Warrior.* An activist, speaker, and thought leader, she is also the founder and president of Together Rising, an all-women-led nonprofit organization that has revolutionized grassroots philanthropy—raising over $20 million for women, families, and children in crisis, with a most frequent donation of just $25. Glennon was named among OWN Network's SuperSoul 100 inaugural group as one of 100 "awakened leaders who are using their voices and talent to elevate humanity." She lives in Florida with her wife and three children.

GlennonDoyle.com
Instagram: @glennondoyle
Twitter: @glennondoyle
Facebook.com/glennondoyle

ABOUT TOGETHER RISING

Founded in 2012 by Glennon Doyle, Together Rising exists to transform our collective heartbreak into effective action. Whether it's pulling children out of the sea outside the refugee camps in Greece, providing a single mother access to breast cancer treatment, or reuniting families separated at the U.S. border—Together Rising identifies what is breaking the hearts of givers and then connects givers' generosity with the people and organizations who are effectively addressing each critical need.

Together Rising has raised over $20 million for people in need with a most frequent donation of $25, proving that small gifts can change the world in revolutionary ways.

Because a few devoted benefactors directly cover all administrative costs, 100 percent of what Together Rising receives from every personal donation goes directly to an individual, family, or crisis. Please consider joining Together Rising's Team Love with a monthly tax-deductible donation of $5, $10, or $25. These donations enable Together Rising to act quickly to deploy life-saving funds in times of crisis.

www.togetherrising.org

Instagram: @Together.Rising

Twitter: @TogetherRising

Facebook.com/TogetherRising